# The Joy

## THE

## OF BEING
## Forgiven

# Andrew Murray

 *Whitaker House*

Unless otherwise indicated, all Scripture quotations are taken from the *King James Version* (KJV) of the Bible.

## THE JOY OF BEING FORGIVEN

ISBN: 0-88368-388-1
Printed in the United States of America
Copyright © 1983 by Whitaker House

Whitaker House
580 Pittsburgh Street
Springdale, PA 15144

4 5 6 7 8 9 10 11 12 13 / 05 04 03 02 01 00 99 98 97 96 95

# CONTENTS

# I

## THE PSALMS

### A Psalm Of David For The Chief Musician

The Book of Psalms is the innermost sanctuary. It is the Holy Place of the sanctuary of the Bible. In the rest of the Bible we receive instruction from God on the way to draw near to Him. In Psalms, God opens the door of His secret dwelling place. He shows us how His believing people come to Him, speak with Him, and enjoy fellowship with Him. There we see the throne of grace surrounded with petitioners. There we learn to pray. There the grace of God is manifested in the most glorious way.

### Praying With God's Words

Similarly, the Book of Psalms is like the lowest class of a nursery school. In the more advanced classes the teacher tells the children what they have to learn. They know how to work independently and only need the teacher's help from time to time. But with the youngest class, who are learning the "A,B,C's," a different method is needed. Every letter must be pronounced and dictated to them. The teacher must put the sounds for them in their mouth, until they learn to pronounce and know them for themselves. This is the way the Lord God deals with us in the Psalms. He comes as the Faithful One, nearer to us than in the rest of the Bible. He gives us the very words we need in order to come to Him. He is aware that we do not know how to pray. Therefore, He comes and tells us what we ought to pray for. When we speak His words, it is with the desire to understand them so that we can feel and pray as He has expressed them. Then He gives us His blessing, and His Spirit makes the words living and powerful in our souls. In these precious Psalms, God's Holy Spirit Himself teaches us to pray.

### Prayers That Meet Our Needs

This book will become more precious to you when you consider *the way* the Lord God has dictated the words so that you can pray them. Has He sent directions from heaven for prayer as if He had ordained them there for us? If that were the case they would not be truly human, nor would they be relevant to our situations on the earth. The Holy Spirit has taught us to speak in the language of men, with the feelings of men, and from the heart of men. The Lord has used men with passions like ours, and sinners like we are, who have experienced every possible condition of human need and sorrow.

God has taught these men by His Holy Spirit to speak these prayers and commit them to writing. Now He offers them to us as a prayer book adapted to our needs. They are adapted to our needs because they come from His Spirit. Therefore they are divine. Yet they are just as human, because they come from those who are our flesh and blood, and are in every way like ourselves. For this reason the Psalms has been precious to sinners who are concerned about their salvation. It will also become precious to you if you earnestly desire to seek after God.

In other books of the Bible much is written about sin and conversion and the conflict of believers. In the book of Psalms you can see and hear the believers themselves—you have the key to their inner chamber. You can see them in their fellowship with God. You hear how they confess sin and ask for forgiveness. You can see how they praise God for His grace and pour out their heart before Him. You can kneel down and pray with them. Your heart will be kindled by their repentance and their faith.

Alone with God in the light of His presence, the writers of the Psalms lay all their life before Him. Like looking in a mirror you can see your life reflected in the concerns, problems and joys expressed in the Psalms. You can see the hidden conflict coming from the sense of guilt, as well as conversion and faith. You can see what it is like to be with a soul in whom God is working.

You will never learn to know sin, especially

your own, until you have learned to agree with the deep confession of the writers of the Psalms. When you have learned to give praise and thanks with the poets of the Psalms, you will learn to glory in God and rejoice in His grace.

For this reason seekers of salvation have always loved the Psalms. For this reason many of the most distinguished saints of God have said that the Psalms become more precious to them the longer they use them.

Think of the Son of God. He taught us to use the Psalms and sanctified them for us. When He was in the heaviest stress of His conflict He cried, "My God, My God, why hast Thou forsaken Me?" (Matthew 27:46). Were the words of the Twenty-second Psalm written to meet His condition? When dying He cried, "Father, into Thy hands I commit My spirit" (Luke 23:46). Was that not a word from Psalm 31:5? If Christ Jesus needed the words of the Psalms to comfort and strengthen Himself in prayer to His Father, how much more must you and I have used these divine prayers to correctly draw near to God.

### Praying With The Psalmist

The blessings that come from using these words are abundant. "The word is nigh thee, saith the Lord, in thy mouth, and in thy heart" (Romans 10:8). Whenever we take God's words and express them, a way is prepared for the Word to get from the mouth to the heart. Through the mouth the Word comes into the heart. You will see that the

8

words of God are the living seeds which germinate, shoot out roots, spring upward, and bear fruit. Your heart is the soil. All you have to do is open it. Then you will see that it is the Word of God that works mightily in the believer.

I invite you to meditate with me on the Fifty-first Psalm. Let us learn to pray this psalm together. Let us think about it verse by verse. Learn it by heart and receive it into your spirit, then speak it before God on your knees. For David this psalm was the way out of the depths of sin to the joy of forgiveness. It was his way to a rich experience of the grace of God. Psalm fifty-one can also bring you and me into this blessing. It will teach you that confession is the road that leads to true forgiveness. Prepare yourself to learn by heart and to pray this psalm. The blessings it will bring you are beyond your present comprehension.

## II

## PSALM 51

*For the Chief Musician A Psalm of David, when Nathan the prophet came unto him, after he had gone in to Bathsheba.*

We find different kinds of psalms in the Psalter of David. There are psalms of thanksgiving for praising and thanking the Lord. There are psalms of instruction to teach us one portion or another of divine truth. There are petitioning psalms where God's help is asked for in the midst of distress or sorrow. And there are repentant psalms where, after confession of sin and guilt, request is made for forgiveness and redemption.

### Why David Wrote This Psalm

The Fifty-first is one of the seven repentant psalms. Indeed, it is the greatest of them all. To understand this particular psalm, we must pay special attention to the situation David was in when he wrote it. The introduction to this psalm gives us some information. David had deeply fallen into sin. He had committed adultery with Bathsheba,

Uriah's wife. Then he tried to conceal his sin. When he did not succeed, he had Uriah put to death. Even this was not the worst aspect of his situation. If he had really confessed his sin, everything might have worked out. Instead, for a whole year his heart remained hardened. Finally, after the birth of David's child, God sent the prophet Nathan to him, and he realized the true nature of his sin. Nathan had drawn from him a sentence of condemnation against a rich man who had robbed a poor man of his only pet lamb. After David himself condemned the man, Nathan exclaimed, "Thou art the man." Then David humbled himself and acknowledged, "I have sinned against the Lord" (see 2 Samuel 12).

The prophet spoke to him in the name of God. "The Lord also has put away thy sin; thou shalt not die" (2 Samuel 12:13). This, however, was not enough for David. He was so grieved about what he had done, that he went to the Lord in deep humility to confess his sin. David begged God to give him divine grace for the forgiveness of sin and renew his heart. This psalm was written to confess his sin and express his need for forgiveness.

I want you to learn to understand this psalm because its lessons are of such great value. There are three elements in the spiritual life which we must know if we are to live and die as believers. We must know: how great our sin is; how we can be delivered from our sins; and how we should live in thankfulness to God for this deliverance.

These lessons concerning our sinful nature, deliverance, and thankfulness are most clearly explained in this psalm. Let us ask God to open our hearts and impress these lessons on our spirit.

## The Magnitude Of Our Sin

The first lesson we must learn is how terrible and wretched our sins are. Think for a moment who David was. He was the man after God's own heart. He was "the man who was raised on high, the anointed of the God of Jacob, and the sweet psalmist of Israel" (2 Samuel 23:1). Think of the wonderful things God did through him and for him. He had been purified through many difficult trials. God had highly honored him, and David had gloriously praised God. Yet look what became of him whenever God gave him over to the desire of his own heart. He fell into intense sin and remained hardened in it for a long time. Nothing but the Word of God by the prophet could bring him to his senses.

I am afraid that there are many among us who do not know what their sins are. Until they know their sins, they cannot really come to the confession of their guilt or experience mercy. They will die in their sin. When it is too late—in eternity itself, they will see what sin was. This is the reason I present this psalm to you. I want to show you the sin of David, and like Nathan, say to you, "Thou art the man."

I want to show you how corrupt the nature of man is. I want to show you how your heart is the source of all sin and makes you capable of all sin. I especially want to show you how the power of sin can blind a man. You are not aware of your sin until the Spirit of God teaches you to know it. You do not know the real nature, the ugliness and the curse of sin, until God makes it known to you. Therefore, come and listen to the prayer of David, a man of God. You will learn what you still do not know about sin and the misery it brings.

## The Deliverance From Our Sin

You must also learn *what glorious deliverance is available from God.* In this psalm you will see that great things must be done in you. David feels he must be washed by God from his sin, and that his transgressions must be blotted out. He also asks that he be purified within, renewed in heart, and that the Spirit of God dwell in him always.

Reader, come with me and you will hear from David what must take place in you. No matter how sinful and helpless you may feel, you have access in prayer to a God who can and will work in you. David's prayer is designed by the Spirit of God to teach you how you must come to God, and what you can expect and receive from God.

## Gratitude From Our Heart

You must also learn *what it means to live a life of thankfulness to God.* You will understand in this psalm how one who is redeemed feels united with God. It is the believer's desire to praise and serve God. It is a joy to tell others what God has

13

done for him. This is not a burden upon him, but a work of love which his heart needs, and which the grace of God makes possible. Grace will sanctify, not only the hidden life of the heart, but the outward life, conversation, and walk. The redeemed soul is known as one who has become an entirely new man. This is brought about by grace, and given to a sinner who has the same feelings and problems as you. Yes, in this psalm you will see a man confessing his sin with the deepest sorrow and anxiety. Then, under the working of the grace of God, he receives redemption. Finally, he glorifies God as a redeemed and emancipated soul.

I want you to join me in the study of this psalm, so you can see how God has made confession the road to forgiveness. You will see how God accomplishes everything you need. You will see that God demands nothing which He does not first give. The service to which He calls you is a blessed, joyful service of willing love. This love is awakened by His love shed abroad in the heart.

## Chapter 1

## THE MERCY OF GOD

*"Have mercy upon me, O God, according to Thy lovingkindness"*—Psalm 51:1a.

In this verse is the key to Psalm Fifty-one. During the long period before David was brought to humiliation by the Spirit of God, he could not pray this simple prayer. Only the person who has been brought to an awareness of sin by God Himself is in a position to use this word in prayer with his whole heart. Only the person who prays it from the heart can truly understand it. David learned to pray this prayer on his knees with a broken heart, in bitter sorrow for his sin. This prayer must be spoken upon the knees with humility and to God. Then it can become a blessing to us and we can make this psalm our own.

### There Is Mercy With God

"Have mercy upon me, O God." We must believe that there is mercy with God. The greatest wonder of His divine being is that with God there is mercy.

15

Here on the earth we give little thought to this great wonder of God's mercy. However, in heaven, people are humbled by the thought of it and never cease to adore and thank God for His mercy. There God is known as the Holy One, and He comes against sin as a consuming fire. In heaven, sin is known for what it is: the shameful rejection of the Perfect One—of His law and love. It is known that man deserves to be rejected by God. Therefore, it is in this mercy of God that glory is seen. Angels do not understand how He could have compassion for our fallen race and that He Himself would pay the ransom for our sin at the cost of the blood of His own Son. The idea that He longs after the ungodly, forgives them everything, and receives them as His children is so great that the angels cannot account for such mercy. David heard that there was mercy with God and he draws near to Him with this prayer. We also must try to understand and believe that there is mercy with God.

## We Need God's Mercy

"Have mercy upon me, O God." We must also feel that we need mercy. Mercy is something that is entirely undeserved. David feels that his sin is so shameful. It makes him guilty in the eyes of the holy God, and he deserves to be condemned. It is not God alone who condemns him. He condemns himself. He feels that he is entirely deserving of the judgment of God. His sin shows how he had withdrawn from God in spite of all the goodness of God toward him. He feels that mercy would be marvelous if he is considered worthy to be made a friend of God. Yes, the true petitioner feels that he needs mercy. Nothing but free grace can be his hope.

## We Must Seek God's Mercy

"Have mercy upon me, O God." We must desire for mercy to be shown to him. David knows that there is mercy, and he feels that he needs mercy, yet this is not enough. He wants God to show that His mercy is intended for him. He knows that the showing of mercy must be a personal action of God toward each person. I know that God is merciful, he cries. The fact that there is mercy for everyone does not satisfy me. I need to know that *God is merciful to me.* Be merciful to me, O God of mercy.

This longing for mercy is in harmony with what God's Word teaches us on these points. The Word always speaks of *finding* mercy, *obtaining* mercy, *receiving* mercy, *partaking* of mercy, and *having* mercy. From God's side it is called *giving* mercy, *showing* mercy. Sin is a personal offense committed against God. Conversion is coming to God to receive redemption from Him so He can show mercy to us by taking away sin.

Many people have mistaken ideas about God's mercy. They comfort themselves with the thought that God is merciful. They have, however, no idea that this will personally affect them. Mercy must be given to them by God and must be experienced in the soul. They forget that there is a work which mercy does for the soul. They forget that God is the Righteous One as well as the Merciful One. Before His righteousness can liberate a single soul, His holy law must be fulfilled. The sinner must partake of the righteousness of Christ and the acquittal of God. Even with the word of mercy on their lips, many go on to meet destruction. This does not happen because there is no mercy with God for him, but because he has never personally experienced the work of divine grace.

Let us review these thoughts concerning mercy. First of all, remember *that there is mercy with God.* Let your soul be filled with the thought that with God there is mercy, and the highest joy of His heart is to show mercy. Furthermore, *you need mercy.* Without mercy you will be eternally miserable. Especially remember *that you must have a personal experience of this mercy.*You must *have* mercy. Without this you cannot rest contentedly. God must do something for you. He must show you mercy. Let God's great mercy and your great misery be the two arguments which cause you to pray this prayer more earnestly. Pray "Have mercy upon me, O God, according to Thy lovingkindness," until you receive mercy.

## Chapter 2

## GOD REMOVES OUR SIN

*"According unto the multitide of Thy tender mercies blot out my transgressions"*—Psalm 51:1b

In the second half of the first verse, David gives a more precise explanation of what he meant in the first part of the prayer, "Have mercy upon me." He knew there was something that mercy could and would do for the sinner. It was his desire to experience this precious work. Therefore he prayed, "Blot out my transgressions."

### Be Specific

The general prayer for mercy is not enough. The Lord wants us to know and say what we want mercy to do for us. The blind man cried, "Jesus, Thou Son of David, have mercy on me" (Mark 10:47). Jesus called him to Himself and asked him, "What wilt thou that I should do unto thee?" (Mark 10:51). He had already prayed for compassion and mercy, but this was not enough. The Lord wanted a specific statement of what His compassion was to do for him. It is not enough for us to be content with a general request for mercy. The Lord will test the sincerity of our desire for mercy by finding out if we know what we want.

Many people pray for mercy and yet receive no answer. Some think that the first work of mercy is to comfort the heart. This is not so. Later in this psalm David prays for comfort and peace. Others believe that the work of mercy consists of changing their heart and their way of life. Later on David asks for this, but it does not happen at first. Others suppose they must ask for mercy and trust that it will take them to heaven when they die. They think that in this life we cannot be sure that we have mercy. David teaches us that this is not what he desired. This is what we should ask God to do for us: "According to the multitude of Thy tender mercies blot out my transgressions."

### God Alone Blots Out Sin

*Our transgressions must be blotted out by God Himself.* This is the conviction which drew David near to God. He feels that transgression must be blotted out. He feels that he is not able to do this work. Mercy must do it for him. Moses said to God, "Yet now, if Thou wilt forgive their sin. . .and if not, *blot me, I pray Thee, out of Thy book which Thou hast written*" (Exodus 32:32). Our sins are also written in God's book. The law of God takes into account every sin we commit. In the account book of heaven, they stand against us

20

as a record of our guilt. David knew there could be no fellowship with the holy, righteous God as long as his guilt was not abolished and blotted out. He knew that mercy could not convert or change the sinner. It could not bring him to heaven, unless his guilt was first blotted out. First, the wrath of God must be appeased. Past guilt must be removed. The sinner must have acquittal and forgiveness of his sins. This is the first work of divine grace. Without this, God the holy Judge cannot receive the sinner into His friendship. Therefore, he prays, "Have mercy upon me. Blot out my transgressions."

Many people remain unacquainted with the holiness of God and the dreadful character of sin. They think that if they repent, live a better life, and pray to God, that God, because of this great change, will receive them. This is not true although change is good. Rather, you should pray to be changed by the Spirit of God. But this is not enough, because it does not get rid of the old guilt. The fact that you want to get rid of your guilt does not cancel it either with God or man. What you must know before all else is the status of the guilt of your former life. Does it remain in God's book against your name? Is it blotted out? Until we know that it is blotted out we can have no real peace.

This is why we must pray the prayer, "Have mercy upon me." The blotting out of guilt is absolutely essential. We cannot work this out by our repentance. God has promised to grant it. His promise is, "I, even I, am He that blotteth out thy transgressions for Mine own sake, and will not remember thy sins" (Isaiah 43:25).

## The Blessings Of Forgiveness

This is what the New Testament calls being "justified." In the parable of the publican he prayed to God, "Be merciful to me a sinner" (Luke 18:13) and he went down to his house justified. This was what grace did for him. This was the answer to his prayer and he went home with forgiveness of his sins. Like David, he could sing when he received this answer to his prayer, "Blessed is he whose transgression is forgiven, whose sin in covered. Blessed is the man unto whom the Lord imputeth not iniquity" (Psalm 32:1,2).

Does this seem too wonderful to believe? Remember that the tender mercies of God are very great. It is on God that David calls. He prays, "According unto the multitude of Thy tender mercies." Come and experience the great, wonderful, and divine element in the grace of God. It will blot out all your guilt at once and remove it completely from God's book. Come and experience the blessing and power of mercy to grant the forgiveness of sins for Jesus' sake.

Chapter 3

# WASHED IN THE BLOOD

*"Wash me thoroughly from mine iniquity"*— Psalm 51:2*a*.

This verse will make the meaning of the preceding chapters clearer. David begs for mercy. He expects the manifestation of it in the forgiveness of his sins. He longs for his transgressions to be blotted out of God's book and taken away from His eyes. But the sin which he looks at weighs heavily upon his soul. It is not only recorded in God's book, but it has stained his conscience and clings to him like a blemish that makes him detestable in his own eyes. Therefore, he prays to be freed from the sense of guilt and from this awareness of inner sin. He knows that this same mercy can erase sin in God's book and in his own conscience. The act of God in heaven is also an act of God in man's own spirit. Therefore, he prays, "Wash me thoroughly from mine iniquity." He knows that the only way his sin can be removed is by a spiritual act of the grace of God. This must wash him of his sin.

## The Symbol Of Washing

Why did David use such an expression for the work which he desired to be accomplished by grace? The ceremonial washings and sprinklings of the Old Testament led him to pray this way. Under the old covenant every priest had to wash himself whenever he offered a sacrifice. Also, any Israelite who had in any way come into contact with something unclean had to first be washed before he could mingle among the other people. David knew that these washings were symbols of what must take place in the heart of man. They were a symbol of cleansing by the blood of Jesus Christ. The New Testament speaks of Jesus as "Him that. . .washed us from our sins in His own blood" (Revelation 1:5). Of believers upon the earth it says, "Ye are washed" (1 Corinthians 6:11). Of the redeemed in heaven it says, "They. . .have washed their robes, and made them white in the blood of the Lamb" (Revelation 7:14). In full light of these expressions let us consider this prayer, "Wash me thoroughly from mine iniquity."

## The Blood Of Jesus

What does it mean to be washed *in the blood of Jesus?* The Word of God teaches us that the sprinkling of blood under the old covenant was a symbol of the cleansing from sin. Everyone who had sinned was guilty of death. But God permitted the Israelites to bring a lamb or another victim to die

24

in his place. Then when the blood of that victim was shed, it was proof that the punishment of death which the man had deserved had been met. When it was sprinkled on the altar, the blood was accepted by God as valid, and the sin was washed away.

So the blood of Christ was shed as the payment for our sins. We are all under the death sentence. We have sinned, and made ourselves guilty according to the law of God. The law has spoken its curse over us as transgressors. It can by no means withdraw its demands until they are met. God would not be righteous if He did not maintain the authority of His law and uphold its power. He would not be a perfect judge if He welcomed transgressors of His law into favor. Therefore, no one can inherit heaven if they are not pronounced clean by the law. And, no one can possibly be pronounced clean who has not fulfilled its demands. No person by himself has been able to do this.

Therefore, the mercy of God steps in between us with the gift of His Son. Christ has fulfilled the demands of the law in our place. He was our representative. He came in our nature to do in our place all that was required of us. He was our surety, who paid the price in our place. He was the Lord of the law but was born *under law* to fulfill its demands. He has honored it by perfect obedience. By dying an accursed death He subjected Himself to its sentence on our behalf. He has borne our punishment. He has taken its curse upon Himself. Because of that He has paid what He had to demand from us. His blood, His soul, and His life is poured out in His death. Like the sacrifice, the outpouring and the sprinkling of His blood is the proof that atonement has been made.

## You Must Be Washed

We should be *washed* in that blood. What does this mean? If someone wants to be cleansed from his sin, it does not help to have a stream of water flow past him. If he does not enter and come in contact with the water, his sin will not be washed away. So it is with the blood of Christ. You must have a personal part in it. Your soul must come into contact with that holy blood in order to experience the power of it. Christ did not come, as many suppose, to abolish the claim of the law, but to fulfill it. The law has a claim upon you, personally and individually, and will ask you if you have obtained the righteousness and atonement of the Lord Jesus. The law will ask: Have *you* been sprinkled and washed with the blood of Christ? If you have been washed, then you are also acquitted. It is not because the law has no claim upon you, but because it sees that Jesus has fully met that claim for you. If you are not washed in that blood, then it does not help you that Jesus has died.

Fellow sinner, realize what must take place within you, or there is no hope for you. The Lord Jesus still says, "If I wash thee not, thou hast no part with Me" (John 13:8). With all your praying, seeking, and all your piety, you will not be saved

26

unless the everlasting God does this spiritual wonder in you—unless you are washed in the blood of Christ. Do not reject the precious blood of Christ any longer. Come to God with the prayer of David, "Wash me thoroughly from mine iniquity."

The blood of Jesus has been shed for you, and God Himself is prepared to wash you in that blood. God Himself by the Holy Spirit will bring your soul into spiritual contact with that divine blood. He will make it possible for you to appropriate and experience the power of that blood. It is the work of God. He will do it. Just believe what the Word says. Believe that the blood of Jesus cleanses you from all sin. Believe that without any worthiness in yourself you can by the attributes of that blood be freed from all your guilt in a moment. Believe that God is sincere when He offers that blood to you. Because of your faith in Jesus' blood let your prayer become more urgent. "Wash me thoroughly from mine iniquity." "Being freely justified by His grace through the redemption that is in Christ Jesus: whom God hath set forth to be a propitiation through faith in His blood" (Romans 3:24,25).

## Chapter 4

## CLEANSED FROM SIN

*"And cleanse me from my sin"*—Psalm 51:2*b*.

David's sin weighed heavily on his soul. Three times he cried out before the Lord to free him from his sin. He did not mean deliverance from punishment. He did not mean being restored to God's favor. It was his sin which was so terrible to him. This was what he wanted God to take away. It is obvious that he deeply felt what sin was because the three utterances he used represent sin in a distinct light.

### Cleansing According To The Law

David saw sin as a *transgression* of the law of God, a violation of the honor and authority of His King and Lord. He calls it *iniquity* according to its inner character, because it was the exact opposite of all that was good, holy, and righteous. He confessed it *as sin*, a condition of disobedience and misery. He had prayed that these would be blotted out of God's book. He wanted to be cleansed of his iniquity. Once again, in view of his sin, David prays for cleansing. He makes known his desire for the redemption which he expects from God's grace. "Cleanse me from my sin."

The word translated *cleanse* is the same word which David found in the laws concerning leprosy in Leviticus 13 and 14. It appears there ten times and is translated to pronounce clean. Let us refer to these passages for the explanation. Whenever someone thought he had leprosy, he had to be brought to the priest. If it was really so, then the priest pronounced him unclean. If it was not this disease, however, then he pronounced him clean. If a leper had been healed of this disease, the priest had to pronounce him clean or unclean. After that he could return again to the temple and have the enjoyment of all the privileges of the people of God. In like manner we see that in the New Testament the word "cleanse" is always used about leprosy. Whenever anyone was cleansed by Jesus, he still had to go to the priest in order to be pronounced clean in the name of God.

## Leprosy Of The Body And Soul

From these and similar passages it is evident that two things were necessary for cleansing. First, the sufferer had to be clean of his leprosy. Then, he must be pronounced clean. In this psalm we find these two elements in the purity which is expected from the grace of God. In verse seven we hear, "Purge me with hyssop, and I shall be clean." This especially refers to being pronounced clean and acquitted from guilt. Later on, in verse ten when we hear, "Create in me a clean heart, O God," this refers to the inner cleansing of the nature and the spirit.

Nevertheless, we see here a distinction between the leprosy of the body and that of the soul. The leper must first be personally clean, and then he is pronounced clean. The sinner, on the contrary, is first pronounced clean, and then becomes, more and more, a partaker of the inward cleansing. The distinction, however, is not as marked as it appears. For the sinner is pronounced clean only by virtue of his union with the Lord Jesus. Jesus the perfectly pure One takes him into His purity. He becomes the guarantee that this purity will be given to him. It is because he is clean in Jesus that he is pronounced clean. Then he becomes more inwardly purified. So the two aspects of purity have one root, namely, "the purity of Jesus." The two are one.

The same grace which pronounced clean also makes clean. The same repentance which desires acquittal also longs for inward purity. In this prayer, "cleanse me from my sin," derived from the law concerning leprosy, David appears to have embraced these two elements together. What he later separates is still united here in this one supreme thought "I want to be free from sin. Take the sin which I have committed away from me. Take away from me the sin which is still hidden within me. Cleanse me from my sin."

It was the work of the priest to cleanse the leper. David wanted to have this priestly action done at the hands of God. He knew that although this cleansing is a hidden, spiritual work it is nevertheless very real. He knew that no repentance, conversion, or change of spirit in life could cleanse him from sin. He knew that there is only one, the Holy One, who is mightier than sin and is in a position to cleanse him. He knew that this God was the God of all grace and would do it. Therefore he prays, "Cleanse me from my sin."

## You Need To Be Cleansed

What David found necessary you also need. He wanted the holy God to stretch out His hand from heaven and touch him and take his sins away from him. Let this also be your prayer. Consider it. Sin is mine, it is upon me, it is in me. The purity which God gives can also be mine, both on me and in me. Just as sin is mine the cleansing must also be mine. Otherwise I may not be redeemed. Make David's prayer your own. Make your own prayer that of the leper who cried, "If Thou wilt, Thou canst make me clean" (Mark 1:40).

If you fail to do this completely, think about your sin like David contemplated his. Read in God's Word how terrible the leper's conditon was (Leviticus 13:45,46). Separated from his fellowmen, from the temple and the service of God, he must continually cry out, "Unclean, unclean!" God ordained this as a symbol of sin. Ask God to help you feel what a deadly, terrible disease consumes your soul. As you wander about, away from God's presence and fellowship with Him, pray,

31

"Cleanse me from my sin."

And when you pray this way, Jesus will also say to you, "I will; be thou clean." The leper went out immediately and was cleansed. Only believe in His power to cleanse, His love which seeks you, and His grace sealed with His blood. Then you will know that the cleansing which you cannot understand now has taken place within you.

Therefore, let this prayer of David become your own. Your sin like his is also very great. For him and also for you, God is the only helper. Let your prayer, like his, be a cry from the whole heart. "Have mercy upon me; wash me; cleanse me from my sin."

Chapter 5

# CONFESS YOUR SIN

*"For I acknowledge my transgressions"*—
Psalm 51:3*a*.

David has prayed for mercy, asked God to blot
out his transgressions, and wash him clean from
the guilt of sin. He now proceeds to say, "For I
acknowledge my transgressions." He helps us to
understand for what reasons and in what spirit he
pleads for mercy. He comes as one who is guilty to
confess his sin. He prays for grace like one in a
sinful condition. Everyone who wants to pray from
the depths of his heart the words of David, "Have
mercy upon me, O God," should confess that he
has sinned.

## Acknowledge You Are A Sinner

This knowledge of sin is necessary preparation
for receiving the mercy of God. We can do nothing
to cover or take away our sin. Besides, God does
not require this from us. God only commands this:
Simply acknowledge the unrighteousness which
you have done. God desires nothing but that we

acknowledge ourselves to be both guilty and lost. We must fall at His feet and confess the terrible condition sin has placed us in. We must confess that we have sinned and that sin has made us deserving of punishment. We must admit we are so sinful that we can do nothing to make ourselves acceptable to God. As someone who is guilty and utterly lost, we must submit to God's sentence. We must confess that it would be a wonderful act of divine grace if we were to be received. It is only when we are brought to this point of confessing we are a sinner, that we will receive mercy. Then we stand in the presence of God in our true condition. Then we can truthfully honor and praise God for His grace.

Many people do not understand this procedure. They think that a change takes place in their hearts when God is persuaded to show them favor. They suppose that, whenever they earnestly repent with a great deal of sorrow and deep conviction, then God will show His grace to them. Therefore, they are always taking a great deal of pain to make themselves, in God's presence, as pious and earnest as they possibly can. They think that in this way they will receive revelation and comfort. This is not God's way. God wants nothing from you except to acknowledge your sin and stand before Him as a guilty sinner. Then you will surely and speedily receive His grace. You are to come as a sinner, one who is ungodly, then forgiveness and life will certainly be granted to you.

## David's Example

The example of David also makes plain to us *man's reluctance to confess his sin*. For a long time David was aware that in the matter of Uriah he was guilty of violating the sixth commandment. In the matter of Bathsheba he had violated the seventh commandment. But, he acknowledges in Psalm 32 that he tried to cover and silence his sin. He knew he had sinned, but he did not know how enormous and wicked the sin was. Otherwise, he would have humbled himself immediately. This state of mind lasted for almost a whole year, until he truly realized his sin. When he could no longer hide his evil deeds, he poured them out and acknowledged them in God's presence.

There are many sinners who in some measure have of a sense of sin. Yet they take pains to forget their sin. They do not intend to sin anymore. With this good resolution they come to God. They think that it will make them too discouraged to think deeply about their sin, so they keep themselves back from really knowing it.

The man who wants to receive grace must be willing to look at his sin and think about it. He must become thoroughly acquainted with it. The more thoroughly he makes the bitter confession, "I acknowledge my transgressions," the sooner he will be able to express the sincere prayer for mercy. When he does this, the sooner he will be prepared to receive grace. He will experience what David says, after he found that suppressing and covering his sin brought him no rest. "I acknowledged my sin unto Thee, and mine iniquity have I not hid. I said, I will confess my transgressions unto the Lord; and Thou forgavest the iniquity of my sin" (Psalm 32:5).

## God Alone Reveals Sin

This incident in David's life also teaches us a lesson regarding the knowledge of sin. God Himself must make our sin known to us. It was only after Nathan the prophet had come to David in the name of God with the word of conviction, "Thou art the man," that he cried out, "I have sinned." Man by nature is so under the power of sin that he can hide it from himself even when he has committed it. This is one of the most dangerous evidences of sin. It blinds the heart. It allows pride to rise and make man unwilling to humble himself. It is the work of God's Spirit to make the soul acknowledge sin.

Many times our conscience makes us afraid of punishment, but this fear is the least element in the knowledge of sin. Sometimes trial, sickness, or fear of death makes a man tremble with the fear of hell. That also is one of the least elements of sin, and a very small indication of the sense of guilt. God may use these things and the fear which they awaken as means to arouse a true knowledge of sin. But they are still beneath the level of this knowledge. I have seen many sick and dying men who prayed for mercy without any true knowledge of what sin was.

God alone can give you a knowledge of sin. Pray, therefore, "Make me to know my transgression and my sin" (Job 13:23). Let it become your earnest desire to know your sin.

Think about your sin. Confess it before God. Think about it in the light of God's Law and Word. Try to think about it as committed against the highest holiness and the eternal love of God. Ask God to send you His Spirit, as He sent Nathan to David, so that you can say, "I acknowledge my transgressions." Do not forget to pray. There can be no real prayer for sin if this attitude is not found in the depths of the heart.

## Chapter 6

## SIN IS A PERSONAL MATTER

*"And my sin is ever before me"*—Psalm 51:3*b*.

In the words "my sin is ever before me" David gives a more precise explanation and confirmation of his confession: "I acknowledge my transgressions." He tells the Lord what kind of knowledge this is. His sin has made such a deep impression upon him that he cannot forget it. It is not just a matter of his understanding. It has seized his heart, so that he can no longer get rid of it. "My sin is ever before me."

### Sin Is Enduring

"My sin is ever before me." This reminds us of the enduring, abiding character of the sense of sin. A knowledge of sin is not a lesson that has to be learned in order that we can forget it again and simply go forward. Instead, it must stay with a man to such an extent that he can never forget it. Whenever a person confesses his sin and then lives in the world, that is a sign that he is still not in earnest about his knowledge of sin. If he understands his sinfulness, it is so shameful and wicked that he becomes filled with conviction. He is continually weighed down under the thought of the great evil he has done. This is what we expect from anyone who has done some terrible deed and then gets insight into its character.

Suppose, for example, someone has committed a murder and then obtains repentance for it. Do we expect him to go on laughing or being joyful? Certainly not, especially if the death sentence has been pronounced on him because of his sin. In like manner when a sinner becomes aware of the greatness of his sin, it becomes something he cannot forget, until he is certain that he has forgiveness. He has sinned against God. He has made himself guilty against the law of God and the love of God. In the midst of all his work and distractions of the world he states, "My sin is ever before me."

This is the great question of his life with which he has to deal. This is the one thought which he dwells on, "I have sinned." Nothing can possibly bring him comfort until God has caused him to know, "Thy sin is forgiven thee." Although one comes to God with all sorts of pious words concerning the compassion of God, the soul still remains in this condition until God Himself takes and blots out the sin. We should never think that sorrow for sin is unneccesary. We should never seek superficial comfort. Knowledge of sin is necessary, because it is the work of God. Every soul must learn to say in the prayer for grace, "My sin is ever before me."

## Sin Is Personal

"My sin is ever before Me." This should further remind us of the *personal* character of a true sense of sin. Those in whom the confession of sin is not deep are always ready to say, "Yes, all men are truly sinners." It is as if the thought of the universality of sin made the guilt of each man less. This consideration tends to lessen the guilt of each particular person.

We imagine there are others who are greater sinners than we are, to whom grace is given. Why should there not be grace for me, too? These are the words of those who are not willing to think much of their own personal sin. They may have some knowledge or some general ideas concerning the greatness of sin, but they do not say, *"My* sin is ever before me." These, however, are the words of the true sinner.

He feels that he personally has to deal with God. He feels that he alone has to deal with God in death, in judgment, and everlasting punishment. It is of little importance whether others join him or not. He sees himself as someone who is condemned and lost in the light of God's law. He truly has neither the time nor the desire to think of others. He cannot ask if the sins of others are greater than his own or not. He finds it sufficient to deal only with himself. "My sin is ever before me." He is sincere in his confession: *"My* sin." While many are doing everything to show that the sin is not their own, he acknowledges it with all his heart.

One person imagines that sin belongs to the devil and he is guilty of it. Another thinks that guilt rests on the world and is dependent upon circumstances. A third, not in words but in his heart, says that sin comes by attributing it to God, who caused men to be born in this condition. But the true sinner cries, *"My* sin." Yes, more than my property, my house, or my family, the sin is my own. It is a part of me. No one can take it from me or out of me except God alone. It is a confession of amazing earnestness. "My sin is ever before me."

### See Yourself As God Sees You

Do you want mercy? Then do not turn away from the painful, humbling side of this confession. Do not consider time or pains too costly in order to make it complete. There will be much you may want to lay aside. But be sure of this, there is nothing that is more important to you than your sin. The first thing God sees in you when He thinks about you or watches your actions is your sin. Since this is true, it is most important that you see yourself as God sees you.

In every prayer for grace which you make, this is what God looks at first. Do you truly desire grace and long for it? He wants to see whether you truly hate and condemn yourself as one who is entirely unclean. Are your sins consistently wrong to you?

41

God looks to see whether you will know as a sinner how to receive and value the redemption that is in Christ Jesus. Therefore, learn this lesson, "My sin is ever before me."

Without this there can be no true repentance, no sincere prayer for mercy, no living faith, no well-pleasing fellowship with God. We are destined for the knowledge and the enjoyment of the redemption of God in our life. In addition we are destined for heaven where we will be praising and enjoying that free grace which has redeemed us.

I ask you to consider these things because I know that there are many who deal too superficially with the confession of sins. They are willing to confess that they are sinners, for all men are in the same position. But, they know nothing of the tremendous importance of this confession. They do not speak about it with shame. They do not pray it before God and on their knees. They say it without really hungering for grace. May God redeem them from their indifference and teach them to cry out with a contrite heart, "Have mercy upon me, O God. My sin is ever before me."

Chapter 7

# SIN IS COMMITTED AGAINST GOD

*"Against Thee, Thee only, have I sinned"*—
Psalm 51:4*a*.

In this verse David confesses the seriousness of his sin. He has commited it against God. As we come to understand this, our knowledge of the real nature of sin increases. Our insight into the reasons why only divine grace can take it away, also increases.

In order to feel this we have to think about how the wickedness of a deed depends on the person against whom it is committed. The same action is considered much worse when it is done against a father instead of a child, and against a king instead of an ordinary subject. This is the seriousness of sin. It has been committed against God.

## The Character Of God

Who is God? God is the Holy and Perfect One, who manifests Himself as a consuming fire against all that is evil. He is the King and the Lawgiver of heaven and earth, whose will is joyfully accomplished throughout the whole heaven. He is the Creator and Upholder, who has a right to expect that His creatures will do what He has created them for. He is the God who in accordance with that right has given us His law, and toward whom we should show obedience. Against this God you have sinned. That is, you have withheld obedience from Him. You have refused to do what He commanded you to do. You have not hesitated to violate and break His holy law.

You have sinned against Him. You have exalted and chosen your will, unjust and perverse as it is, above His will. You have said that the counsel and the will of Satan is more attractive to you and has more influence on you than the will of God. You have robbed God of His glory. You have opposed Him. You have attacked Him in His honor. You have dishonored this great and infinite God. You, a poor worm of the dust, have confronted and insulted the high and holy One before whom angels bow down.

And since God is the Lawgiver and the Proprietor of the unverse, He cannot endure sin. He must maintain His right in the universe. Every transgression of His law violates that right. The terrible wrath of God is kindled in order to maintain it. Against this God you have sinned. What do you think? The moment a man sees this God in His greatness, it becomes self-evident that it is that which startles and bruises his soul. "Against Thee, Thee only, have I sinned." Oh what have I done? I have rebelled against this God, the highest perfection. I have dared to provoke His wrath and curse Him. This God, without whom I cannot live, I have made my enemy.

There is still one thought which makes all this more bitter. The God against whom I have sinned is the God of love. He has not only shown me His goodness in the thousand blessings of this life, but He is also the God of love and the Lord of grace who has revealed His Son Jesus Christ in His eternal glory. And I have been such a child of hell that I have dared to sin against this God. I have despised His Son and turned my back on Him. What an inexpressible bitterness there is for the person who truly feels this when he confesses, *"Against Thee, Thee only,* have I sinned."

## Sin Against God

It is this that makes sin so terrible. It is this that makes it so impossible for man to get rid of his sin. The reason for this is that sin is an act of rebellion against the holy God. And, man is not in a position to recall this sin or take it away. Every sin is an assault against God's law and a violation of it. Nothing that man is able to do can possibly erase one single sin that has been committed. Sin has been committed against God. He has observed and noted it. It has attacked Him. He alone can say if He will forgive it. He alone has the power to blot it out and annul it.

Yes, the sin has been committed against God and must be accounted for. Once again, this is the terrible element of sin that is expressed in the confession, "Against Thee, Thee only, have I sinned." Yet how little thought is given to this fact. Even in the case of outright sinners, they think very little of the fact that they have sinned against themselves and their own happiness. They also think very little about what should cause them the greatest concern, namely, the fact that they have sinned against God.

Make this a matter of much prayer, because you will have to deal with God. On judgment day you will meet Him face to face. If you have not thoroughly learned to feel it, then you will experience, to your everlasting horror, what having sinned against God is. Even here it is sorrowful and painful to make confession. But it is better to be humbled here than be condemned forever. Do not allow yourself to be distracted from your attempt to make this confession.

There are thousands of so-called Christians who know nothing of this conviction of sin. Many will say to you that you must not make yourself too anxious about sin, but I feel obligated to tell you that you have reason to worry about your sin. You have sinned against God, and He is a consuming fire. Your sin is so great, the danger so threatening, that it is highly unreasonable not to be anxious about sin. You have sinned and God has spoken His sentence of wrath upon you. It is sheer stupidity to look for rest and comfort before you know that God has taken away your sins.

At any moment His anger could explode against

you. Hurry to Him with the confession, "Against Thee, Thee only, have I sinned." And if your heart does not feel it as deeply as it should, beg Him to work it out in your heart. The Spirit who taught David the word will also teach you to say, *"Against Thee, Thee only, have I sinned."*

## Chapter 8

# GOD'S JUDGMENT AGAINST SIN

*"Against Thee, Thee only, have I sinned, and done this evil in Thy sight: that Thou mightest be justified when Thou speakest, and be clear when Thou judgest"*—Psalm 51:4.

David is perfectly sincere in every confession that he makes. Under the pressure of what he is feeling, he confirms a second time, "Against Thee, Thee only, have I sinned." Now there follows another word, "And done this evil in Thy sight: that Thou mayest be justified when Thou speakest, and be clear when Thou judgest." In these words he presents the reason why he openly admits his sin. He desires to approve the sentence of God and acknowledge that His verdict concerning him could be nothing except the righteous judgment which he deserved. He has made confession of his guilt so that God can be justified in His speaking and clear in His judging. The person who prays sincerely for grace will try to be inspired with this same feeling. Let us look at what this really means.

48

# The Nature Of God's Judgment

Consider the terrible nature of God's judgment. Every one is cursed if they do not continue in the things written for them to do. This is the sentence of the Lawgiver. He explains that every single transgression of His law brings His curse on man. He does not investigate the excuse which man might make. The sentence is not changed. "The soul that sinneth, it shall die" (Ezekiel 18:20). This word will be spoken to every transgressor on judgment day: "Depart from me, ye cursed, into everlasting fire" (Matthew 25:41).

The person who is truly aware of his sins admits that this sentence is not too heavy or strict. It is not more than he deserves. He acknowledges that God is perfectly entitled to deal this way with sin and condemn it. However intolerable the judgment of God may be, the sinner feels that it is not too severe. He confesses that he has sinned against God so that he may confirm the truth that God is righteous. This was David's confession. There was no reason for him to plead for any other sentence. If he were still to be received, it must only be by free, undeserved grace. He was, in truth, sincere about his sense of guilt. He must have seen its detestable, inferior nature differently than most men, in order to be able to speak this way. He felt that the sentence of God was something terrible.

In his anguished soul which he had endured for a long time, he had experienced how terrible it feels to be abandoned by God. Yet he acknowledges the righteousness of the sentence and yields himself to it. This is surely something beyond man's nature. Such a sense of guilt and condemnation must have been formed in him by the Spirit of God.

## David Offers No Excuse

This becomes more apparent when we think about man's tendency to excuse himself. David had served God from his youth, and he had suffered more than any other of God's servants for God's name and honor. God Himself testified that he had walked with Him with a perfect heart. The Lord at a later time allowed it to be stated in His Word that He had strengthened Jerusalem "Because David did that which was right in the eyes of the Lord, and turned not aside from any thing that He had commanded him all the days of his life, save only in the matter of Uriah the Hittite" (1 Kings 15:5). Must this one sin be considered so severely? An earthly king would certainly forgive a single transgression committed by a faithful servant. God, the merciful and gracious One, should also forgive this sin without being asked. There was no necessity for confession.

This is the way that people speak and think. They do not know the terrible reality of God's holiness and His judgment on sin. They do not know that every single sin, although it is only one, is a violation of God's law and an injury to His honor. It is a proof of rebellion in the heart and that it must be avenged. David bows himself before God, not because God is too strong for him. No, that is not the reason. David had such a view of the authority of God that he approved of God's sentence. He saw how good it was that the law of God should be maintained. He saw how necessary it was that the glory and honor of God should be established. Under the power of that feeling, he confesses his sin against God alone. He does this so that he can give honor to God and acknowledge that He was justified in His speaking and clear in His judging.

## The Spirit Convinces Us Of Sin

This feeling is certainly beyond man's nature. Such a sense of guilt and condemnation had to have been formed in him by the Spirit of God. And the Lord has permitted this verse in His Word, so that we see what happens to a man who is on the way to genuine repentance and conversion. What a different experience this is from the superficial confession of sin with which most people are content. They confess that they are sinners, but they see their sin as a weakness, a flaw in their character, a misfortune. They sympathize with the sinner, but they are unconcerned about the honor of God. The poor sinner must be comforted, but whether the honor of God's law is maintained does not concern them.

That is not the kind of repentance the Spirit of God works in the heart. If a person is truly convinced of sin by the Spirit of God, he does not merely think of himself and what concerns him. His great sorrow is that he has dared to commit sin against a holy God, whose law is perfect. His great concern is to restore what he has destroyed. Since he can do nothing else, he lays down at the feet of God and yields to Him the only honor that he can now give. He acknowledges that God is righteous in His judgment.

Have you learned to know your sins? God has given His law to convince you of sin, "that every mouth be stopped, and all the world may become guilty before God" (Romans 3:19). Have you already given God this honor, trembling as you did it? Have you humbled yourself before Him as worthy of the judgment of God? The person who does this and admits he is a sinner, he alone can receive mercy. See to it that you really know and confess your sin. Without this there is no grace. Humble yourself under the mighty hand of God, and He will exalt you.

Chapter 9

# OUR SINFUL NATURE

*"Behold, I was shapen in iniquity; and in sin did my mother conceive me"*—Psalm 51:5.

David's confession of guilt does not end with the sin against God which he had committed. He realized that his whole nature was completely impure from his birth. From his youth the grace of God had marvelously preserved him from sin. His whole life had been devoted to God's service. But here he immediately becomes the prey of temptation and makes himself guilty of terrible sin against God. His earlier life of purity cannot comfort him, and instead, increases the bitterness of his grief. He feels his heart must be terribly corrupted. The power of sin in him must be greater than he imagined. Having received so much from God how could he possibly have sinned like this.

## Realizing Your True Nature

All at once the root of this sin has come to the surface. For a long time the grace of God had preserved him. He had almost forgotten that he was just as corrupt as everyone else. Now he is aware of his sinful nature, and he comes before God with the confession of his inborn corruption. This one sin does not call for punishment, "But, my whole nature is impure!" he cries. "Since sin is always present, I am a sinner who needs God's grace." Or, as David expresses in Psalm 51: "Behold, I was shapen in iniquity; and in sin did my mother conceive me."

The inborn corruptness of our nature is an important element in the true confession of sin. How perverted are the ideas of those who appeal to that fact to excuse their sin. There are many who even do this when they confess their sin. They think that since they are sinful by nature the guilt of their sin is not as great. They cannot help being sinful, because they were born this way. This is proof that they still know nothing of the real disgust of sin.

Instead, they should be so ashamed of their sinful nature and rebellion toward God that it would embarrass them to remember that they are one with their ancestors in sin. In view of the unity of the whole human race, they would see that God put all of us to the test in Adam. This thought should cause such shame that they would be silent in the dust before God. The confession of this inborn corruption and feeling of shame is a necessary element in the true confession of sin.

Man must come to see himself as God sees him. Man only looks at what is visible to him. When he does not commit many external sins, he thinks that his sinful nature is not as cursed as that of the open sinner. David was almost trapped in this error. However, when he sinned, he realized that he had the seeds of all ungodliness in his heart, and it was grace alone that preserved him from developing these evil seeds. If we truly believe this, then those who have been kept from ungodly ways by a Christian upbringing should present themselves in all sincerity alongside the greatest sinners. They should feel that they are on the same footing as sinners in God's sight. For this reason the confession of natural corruption is necessary to the true confession of sin.

## The Only Solution—Divine Grace

If I have only committed individual sins, then I can try to compensate for them. However, if I am inwardly corrupt, then every attempt to pay for them is useless and vain. Every good effort becomes stained with sin, and I need free, divine forgiveness. Then I realize that I need not only forgiveness of sins but also renewal of my heart. David united these two blessings in this psalm. As the confession of this inward and outward corruption becomes deeper, the surrender to Jesus and His grace is more complete and abundantly glorified.

It is not just the longing and reception of grace that depends upon this confession. Greater insight into the plan of divine grace comes from our confession. When I see that my misery has its roots in my kinship to the first Adam, then I see how my new union with the second Adam (Jesus) redeems me completely from it. When I understand how the fall of Adam destroyed me because I am born of him and receive his life, I learn to understand how the obedience of the second Adam restores me, because I become one with Him. I am born of Him, and I obtain a part in His life. The all-sufficiency of the divine plan of redemption is made clear to me. I know how to seek my salvation in daily fellowship with that love which flows from God. From every point of view it is clear that the sincere repentant person must confess the entire corruption of his nature from birth.

Have you realized and acknowledged this corruption of your nature? Have you learned to see yourself as one who is entirely impure? Do you regard yourself as loathsome in the eyes of God? Do you see yourself so impure inside that you are good for nothing except to be thrown out?

Are you ashamed of your origin? Does it suprise you that God still loves such an impure creature? Have you turned away from every attempt to improve yourself or make yourself acceptable to God? Do you believe that only God's power is able to renew you? If you feel that you still lack a thorough knowledge of your sin, ask God for it. He can give it to you by His Holy Spirit.

Chapter 10

# BE HONEST WITH GOD

*"Behold, Thou desirest truth in the inward parts"*—Psalm 51:6*a* .

The confession of his sin taught David how to expose its origin. From his birth, his heart has been impure. This leads him to think of God as the searcher of the heart. Before God's eyes, this inward corruption makes him worthy of rejection even when he does not openly commit any sinful deeds. He feels that in his confession of sin he must not leave this out. The God he deals with is a God who desires truth in the inward parts. In our prayer for mercy, it is also important for us not to overlook this word. It will teach us lessons of the greatest importance.

## Be Honest With Yourself

God desires truth in the inward parts. This thought calls us to earnest, godly fear in our awareness of sin. By our nature we dwell more on the outward manifestation of sin than on its hidden source. Whenever the outward life is religious and unblamable because of Christian upbringing or favorable circumstances, many people flatter themselves with the thought that their heart is also right. They feel that although they still have many sins, the heart is not quite as bad as has been said. They do not regard themselves as ungodly enemies of God. When God's Word uses such expressions, they feel it could not possibly mean they are like that. If they only knew how the Lord proves and searches the heart, they would think otherwise. The Holy One sees the indwelling corruption of the heart. There is no man that does good; no, not one. The holy God requires truth in the inward parts. The service He receives must be completely true and and in full agreement with His holy law. Love for God must fill the whole heart. If anything is lacking, then we stand guilty and condemned before God. He cannot be content with less than perfect holiness. This is a terrible thought for the convicted soul. God desires truth in the inward parts.

However, many people experience a superficial conversion and allow themselves to be deceived. For example, there is some anxiety about sin and questions about grace whenever someone is sick, but they are soon comforted. These feelings of conviction can be easily awakened and also very lightly laid to sleep again. They desire the help of God without being prepared to abandon everything in actual life. The heart is deceitful above all things. Through the pious appearance of religion, people many times deceive themselves. If they would only realize that God searches the deepest recesses of the soul. Then, this word of David's would be a word of heartbreaking power and at the same time a word of healing and quickening.

## God Desires Honesty

"Thou desirest truth in the inward parts." This thought gives hope and comfort to those along the road to forgiveness. God will have nothing less from the convicted soul. The grace of God will require nothing more from the repentant person. I learn to see myself as guilty and worthy of condemnation. In me there dwells no good thing. How, then, can I arrive at truth in the inward parts? How can this thought give me comfort?

It comes in these ways. The person who knows himself as lost by nature must present himself to God as he really is. He who comes to God with the acknowledgment of his sin comes in truth. This is the sincerity of which the Word of God speaks. There are many who imagine that sincerity before God means perfection and sincere dedication of themselves to the service of God. However, the anxious sinner should present himself to God and confess himself to be just what he is. The person who confesses his sin certainly receives mercy. God desires truth in the inward parts. The person who desires forgiveness, and is honest with God, can rejoice in receiving salvation.

When you appear before God, do not try to present yourself as one who is holy. Do not appear before Him with an attitude of piety. Instead, confess what you think, feel, and do. Hide nothing from the Lord. Do not try to cover up your sin. Acknowledge the whole truth about your sinful condition. God desires truth and will not withhold His grace from you.

## Honesty Results In Truth

After we have received mercy, we must continue to be honest with God. God desires truth in the inward parts. The person who has been given grace is aware of the deceit and unfaithfulness of his heart. In faith, love, prayer, and dedication to God's service, he discovers that he is still not capable of serving the Lord with the whole heart and in perfect truth like he desires.

Many times the believer is afraid that his soul will bend under pressure. Then he finds in God's Word this glorious promise: "I will direct their work in truth, and I will make an everlasting covenant with them" (Isaiah 61:8). He begins to see that this is also a part of God's plan and promise to confirm and bring to perfection the work of grace He has begun. "Thou desirest truth in the inward parts." This gives us grounds to plead with God to work out that process in which He delights. This word of David becomes the source of the most glorious expectations.

Beloved, in your use of this Psalm and in your fellowship with God, let this verse be the fundamental element of your prayer. Always meet with God as a God who desires truth in the inward parts. In your confession of sin, in your beliefs, in your whole existence let truth in the inward parts be your desire, as it is God's desire.

If you find that there is nothing good in you, that the more you strive after the truth the less you find it, be assured that the acknowledgment of your struggle is already the truth which God desires. If you long for this truth from Him who desires it and who takes delight in giving it, it will be given to you.

Chapter 11

# THE SOURCE OF SPIRITUAL WISDOM

*"And in the hidden part Thou shalt make me to know wisdom"*—Psalm 51:6*b*.

"And in the hidden part Thou shalt make me to know wisdom." This appears to be a transition from the confession of sin to the prayer of redemption. God desires truth in the inward parts. David is led to this thought by the confession of his inborn sin. It was not only his transgression but also his very nature that made him worthy of rejection before God. He cannot by nature stand before the holy searcher of hearts, who desires truth in the very depths of the heart. But this thought leads him back again to God, who alone has the power to bestow truth in the inward parts.

## God Alone Gives Wisdom

The very fact that has brought David low, that God cannot be content with less than truth, also lifts him up again. If the grace of God receives him, then it will give him nothing less. In the hidden parts, God makes him to know wisdom.

Here, in the midst of his prayer, is an expression of the hope that God will make known to him the way to be redeemed from sin. As deep and penetrating as the power of sin was, so will be his knowledge of grace. He trusts that spiritual insight into the way of redemption will be communicated to him by God.

In this psalm we have already seen the explanation of the washings and sprinkling of the blood of the temple service and the spiritual significance of the Old Testament sacrifices. The connection between the forgiveness of sins and the renewing of the heart is presented in his prayer as clearly as anywhere else in the Old Testament. His hope was not in vain. "In the hidden part Thou shalt make me to know wisdom."

This verse teaches us that the true knowledge of the way of grace must be sought from God Himself. He alone can make you know hidden wisdom. Human knowledge of grace which we obtain by the use of our understanding is not sufficient. We did not say that this knowledge is not necessary. But, this knowledge is not enough. There is a great lack of this knowledge, even the intelligent understanding of grace.

## Knowledge Is Not Enough

Many people have an imperfect idea of what grace is and how it redeems the sinner. They do not understand what the blotting out of transgressions, the washing away of unrighteousness, and the cleansing of sin is. Many are unclear about man's sinful nature. It is of supreme importance that clear beliefs be acquired concerning these points. For without clear knowledge, faith cannot be clear, powerful, and joyful. "Do you *understand* what you read?" was the first question asked by the preacher of the gospel. "Do you *believe* with all your heart?" is the second. Such an intelligent understanding of grace is of great value.

However, this is not enough. It is possible that one can have an almost perfect knowledge of God's Word and yet be lost. When we have clear insight into the way of the truth of God, we still run the risk of becoming content with knowledge. When one who is indifferent begins to be earnest, and then obtains an insight into God's wonderful redemption, such knowledge sometimes brings him great joy. When he begins to obtain a correct idea of the plan of redemption in Christ, His atonement, God's righteousness, and the new birth, he is filled with admiration and gladness.

Then he runs the great risk of resting in his feelings. He recognizes this difference in himself compared to the time when he was ignorant. A great change has taken place in him, yet it may be that he has not yet experienced an inward spiritual knowledge of redemption. When seeking to understand the way of grace in this psalm, it is very important that we deeply depend upon God. With every verse we must pray, "Lead me in Thy truth, and teach me: for Thou art the God of my salvation" (Psalm 25:5). He should continually use, for example, the prayers of Psalm 25 and

Psalm 119 in order to obtain divine instruction of the Spirit in this hidden wisdom.

## Depend Solely Upon God

It is amazing to think that a person can be occupied with divine truths and yet still be lost. Such an idea could make us completely discouraged. It would if we were not able to say in this prayer, "In the hidden parts *Thou shalt make me* to know wisdom." God gives the wisdom. This is our only security and is the only answer we can give to the question: How do we know if we have spiritual knowledge of grace? The Lord can and will reassure you of this.

Conversion, like faith, is not a work that you must do. It is not something you can look back on and say, "That is well done." No, the innermost part of conversion and faith consists of coming *to God* and surrender *to God.* It consists of receiving *from God* the *living God,* grace to be worked out by Him. It consists of being washed and purified from sin by Him. It is at this point in Christianity that many are so deficient. They do not know that in grace the principle element is coming into contact with the living God. We must experience the power of the Almighty.

True Christianity is a divine and spiritual thing. The whole work from beginning to end is a wonderful work of the Holy Spirit in the soul. The first desire for grace and spiritual wisdom, the growing sense of sin and faith in the blood of Jesus, are worked into the soul by God. If you are seeking to walk in David's footsteps in this Psalm, go to God with every verse. In every confusing experience throw yourself on God. Ask of Him step by step and word by word to fulfill this promise in you, "In the hidden parts Thou shalt make me to know wisdom."

Chapter 12

# CLAIMING YOUR CLEANSING

*"Purge me with hyssop, and I shall be clean"*—Psalm 51:7*a* .

David has confessed his sins. Now, the prayer for redemption and cleansing follows.

## Ceremonial Cleansing

In order to understand this verse we must look at Numbers 19. There we find this word "purify" as many as seven times as the ceremony of cleansing is described in detail. Whenever anyone touched a dead body, he was considered unclean. Death was the punishment and the curse of sin. Because of this every Israelite who touched a dead body must be considered unclean. He was not permitted to come to the tabernacle. In this way he showed how fellowship with sin and death separate us from God. Only after he had been purified and washed could he be clean again. This is described to us in that chapter. A red heifer had to be burned and its ashes kept in reserve. If anyone became unclean, then the ashes were put in water.

A bunch of hyssop was dipped in it, and the unclean person sprinkled with it. After he washed himself with water, he was clean again. Then, he was purified with hyssop.

In the book of Hebrews this ceremony is definitely mentioned as a type of purification by the blood of Jesus. We read in Hebrews 9:13,14, "For if the blood of bulls and of goats, and the ashes of an heifer sprinkling the unclean, sanctifieth to the purifying of the flesh: how much more shall the blood of Christ, who through the eternal Spirit offered Himself without spot to God, purge your conscience from dead works to serve the living God?"

David already knew that a spiritual purification was represented in this ceremony. He prayed that God might fulfill it in him. He felt that his sin had brought him under the power of death. David was unprepared to serve the living God until he was first cleansed by God Himself. The light of the New Testament, and especially this word from Hebrews, shows us that this purification can only take place by the blood of Christ. Let us look at what David's prayer, illumined by the Word of God, can teach us.

### Cleansing Is Essential

First of all, it teaches us how essential this cleansing is. It is written in Numbers 19:20: "But the man that shall be unclean, and shall not purify himself, that soul shall be cut off from among the congregation, because he hath defiled the sanctuary of the Lord." God is a holy God. Nothing stained with sin can stand before Him. Even a person who merely touched a dead body could not enter into His temple. The impossibility of any fellowship between God and sin is represented under the old covenant by this external strictness. The one who remains in impurity is condemned to death. If he wants to please God and draw near to God, he must allow himself to be purged with hyssop.

God had, in a wonderful way, prepared a sacrifice and water for cleansing. There was no alternative but to be purified with hyssop or cast out from the congregation of the Lord. In the New Testament it is no different. God is the holy One. Sin cannot have fellowship with Him. God is the living God. Death cannot approach Him. Our sins are great and we cannot blot them out. Even our good works are dead works. They bear in themselves the token of sin and the death of the corrupt nature from which they come. The person who is not purified in the way appointed by God, through the sacrifice commanded by God, will be cut off from the congregation.

Nothing you can do, nor any change you make can restore your access to God. Only one thing is necessary. You must be cleansed by God Himself. Otherwise you will not enter His heaven. Let this prayer of David become your own, "Purge me with hyssop, and I shall be clean."

## Cleansing Is Available

David's prayer teaches us that this purifying is available to us. The Spirit of God taught David to pray in harmony with what the temple services taught. The New Testament says to us, "How much more shall the blood of Christ. . .purge your conscience from dead works to serve the living God" (Hebrews 9:14). Yes, it is the blood of Christ that can cleanse us. The red heifer was killed and burned. Its blood was sprinkled on the tabernacle. The water of purifying made from the ashes of this sacrifice could not cleanse anyone.

Jesus is the perfect sacrifice. He died for our sins. He has overcome the power of sin and of death and made it impotent. He has entered with His blood into the Holy Place. You can also be purified and cleansed. Draw near to God with the humble prayer that He will purge you, sprinkle you with this blood, and cause you to experience the power of it. He will do it. The blood of Jesus will cleanse you from all sin.

If by faith you seek to appropriate His blood, the Spirit of God will give you the assurance that God has taken away all your sin. Go to the fountain of Jesus' blood. Present yourself to God praying, watching, trusting. By faith you will know that you are clean.

You will know that you are pure. Your heart will not be so holy that you cannot commit sin anymore, but it will be so purified by the blood that sin is no longer accounted to you. You are no

70

longer burdened with it. You are so purified by the Spirit which is imparted with the blood, that you have a clean heart on which the law of God is written and lives. Jesus said to His disciples, "He that is washed needeth not save to wash his feet, but is clean every whit; and ye are clean" (John 13:10).

Let David's prayer become your own. "Purge me, and I shall be clean." The more earnestly you express that first word with your eyes on Jesus, "Purge me," the more powerfully the Spirit of God will also apply that second word to you, *"I shall be clean."*

## Chapter 13

## PERFECTLY PURIFIED

*"Wash me, and I shall be whiter than snow."*—Psalm 51:7*b*.

The prayer to be washed, which is also in verse two, is repeated once more. This time an explanation of great importance is added to it. David says to the Lord what he believes. The wonderful power of that washing will be, "Wash me, and I *shall* be whiter than snow." The prayer for grace and forgiveness is prayed by many people, but they do not know the answer they ought to expect. They do not believe that the prayer will be gloriously heard. They do not believe that we will be able to draw near to God with the absolute certainty of being whiter than snow.

In order to understand this prayer thoroughly, we must look at this phrase, "Whiter than snow." It does not refer to the inward renewal and purifying of the heart. David does not say that when he is washed he will be perfect and will never commit sin. The person who has been washed clean may always fall again into the mire and become soiled.

Grace gives an inward purity. It does not come at once in perfect form, but gradually step by step.

David speaks about this later when he prays for a clean heart. What he speaks about here is that freedom from guilt which everyone receives with the forgiveness of sins. When God forgives sins, He forgives at once and perfectly. At the moment when God forgives sins, the soul, in His eyes and according to His holy law, is without a spot and entirely clean. As Jesus said to Peter, "He that is washed is clean every whit" (John 13:10). Or, he is "whiter than snow."

## Purified For Heaven

"Wash me, and I shall be whiter than snow." Everyone of us should make this prayer his own. There are some strong arguments that will urge you to take this step. Nothing less than this can keep you pure. You will not be satisfied with less. We have said before that the law of God stands at the gate of heaven and guards the entrance to it. It does not let anyone in who is not *whiter than snow.*

That is the holiness of God and the perfection of the angels. Anything that is less clean and less holy is not permitted in heaven. If there is one single stain in you, the law will reject you. All heaven will throw you out. On judgment day when God's justice flashes out to consume everything stained with sin in fire—nothing that is not "whiter than snow" will stand before a holy God.

73

## Purified Perfectly

Furthermore, nothing less than perfect purifying is offered to you. If you had to do the purifying of yourselves you would soon lose hope. God says, "For though thou wash thee with nitre, and take thee much soap, yet thine iniquity is marked before Me" (Jeremiah 2:22). Instead of this, God has prepared all that is necessary for your salvation. When God forgives, He forgives perfectly. "As far as the east is from the west, so far that He removed our transgressions from us" (Psalm 103:12). The washing of the soul is God's work, an act of God's holy and all-prevailing grace. He is in a position to make it "whiter than snow." It is the blood of Jesus in which we are washed. The power of divine holiness, found in that precious atoning blood, has the power to make whiter than snow.

In other words, the atonement of Jesus Christ is perfect. His righteousness is perfect. His merit is infinite. If His righteousness is attributed to me, I obtain it perfect and entire. If I have part in the Lord Jesus, my Surety, then I have Him completely. Christ is not divided. I am in Him. I have His full righteousness, or I am not in Him and have no part in it. When Jesus bore the curse with us, it was not attributed to Him and laid upon Him according to the measure of His merit and worthiness. It was according to ours. Before God we are endowed with grace along with Jesus. His righteousness is bestowed on us, not according to our merit, but according to that of Jesus. It was an act of divine righteousness that Jesus came as a man to take on Himself our full curse. In like manner, it is an act of God's righteousness that we can come to Him in Jesus to take for ourselves the complete righteousness of Jesus.

Jesus is identified with us as one upon whom the curse must rest. He who believes in Him is one with Jesus and is treated as such. He is accepted in Him and is "whiter than snow." God sees us in Christ. Our sins are entirely and completely forgiven. We are altogether acceptable to Him. He fulfills to us the word, "Though your sins be as scarlet, they shall be as white as snow; though they be red like crimson, they shall be as wool" (Isaiah 1:18). Therefore, let everyone pray, "Wash me, and *I shall be whiter than snow.*" God has offered us nothing less than this.

## The Blessings Of Being Purified

Nothing less than this purifying can bring you full peace. There are many who are seeking peace with God in their own activity, endeavors, and experiences. But they cannot find stable, full peace—the peace which Jesus gives and passes all understanding. Only when we can speak that word by faith, "I shall be clean, I shall be whiter than snow," do we know what it means to say, "Blessed is he whose transgression is forgiven, whose sin is covered" (Psalms 32:1). Only then do we know what is meant by singing, "Bless the Lord, O my soul. . .who forgiveth all thine iniquities" (Psalm

103:2,3). Then our conscience can obtain full peace in view of God and sin, law and the curse, and death and judgment. This happens because the blood of Jesus makes "whiter than snow." The soul rejoices with a joy that is unspeakable and full of glory.

Nothing less than this must be your desire. Lay aside your own prayers and thoughts about what God is to do for you. Learn to pray as the Holy Spirit taught David, "Wash me, and I shall be whiter than snow." Keep these words in your heart. Speak them continually before God in prayer. Make them your continual desire. You will obtain a richer blessing than your prayers have brought you for years.

*Receive this blessing by faith.* This grace is offered to you in Christ. Believe that through Him this purifying is prepared for you. Believe in Him, and you will not only ask with confidence, but you will firmly believe God is doing it. He washes me, and I am whiter than snow. Draw near to Him and take the blessing out of His hand.

Chapter 14

# THE JOY OF BEING BROKEN

*"Make me to hear joy and gladness; that the bones which Thou hast broken may rejoice"*—Psalm 51:8.

David does not simply want forgiveness. He desires more. He also wants joy, gladness, and rejoicing. To him this is a portion of the grace which he asks for and expects will fill his heart with gladness.

There are many people who think they are too unworthy to expect such a blessing of joy from God. They are content to be miserable and depressed all their life, if they can hang onto the hope of one day getting to heaven. To ask for joy and gladness on earth as well is a thing they feel too unworthy to expect. They think this is humility. No, they always want to measure grace according to their own merits, and that is not real grace.

## The Joy Of Forgiveness

David gives us the example of how we are to

know God better, and how to cherish the riches of His grace. He knows that when God forgives, He forgives completely. When He receives anyone again, He receives him with His whole heart. The Lord does not want any cloud separating Him and the believing soul. He wants that soul to know that he is completely restored to His favor. He is restored as completely as if he had never committed sin and can now rejoice with confidence in the forgiving love of God. David knew this. Although he had fallen amazingly low, he is not afraid to ask for entire restoration to the love of God when he asked for grace. "Make me to hear joy and gladness; that the bones which Thou hast broken may rejoice."

Everyone who studies this psalm should understand that he is entitled to ask for nothing less than joy and gladness. God desires this on the part of His people. "Rejoice in the Lord alway: and again I say, Rejoice" (Philippians 4:4). Jesus also desires it. "These things have I spoken unto you, that My joy might remain in you, and that your joy might be full" (John 15:11). The glory of the reward, the love and goodness of God entitle us to expect that forgiveness will transmit joy.

This joy and gladness came when David received what he prayed for, the cleansing of his sins. Yes, it was from the forgiveness of his sins that he expected such gladness. It was always the sense of sin that had grieved and pained him terribly. As long as he had no certainty concerning this blessing, he could have no peace. But when David knew that God was reconciled to him and his sins were blotted out of God's book he was glad. When he knew that he was washed whiter than snow and restored to God's favor no wonder he expected his heart to be filled with joy and gladness. Because of this David prayed that the word of forgiveness spoken to his soul would cause him to hear joy and gladness.

How different this attitude is from those who pray for a short time, and then seek their joy in the world because they know nothing of the joy of God. How different it is from those who pray for forgiveness and do not believe that this blessing can fill them with joy. How different it is from those who seek for the fountain of joy only in themselves or in some wonderful change of heart or holiness in their life. Learn from David that at the very moment you come to the blood of Jesus to receive forgiveness, you can be filled with the joy of God. "Blessed is he whose transgression is forgiven, whose sin is covered" (Psalm 32:1). To the sinner Jesus says, "Be of good cheer; thy sins be forgiven thee" (Matthew 9:2).

## Brokenness Brings Joy

But, why is it that so many never receive this gladness? This verse of psalms points out the true reason. When David says, "That the bones *which Thou hast broken* may rejoice," he reminds us how terrible his conviction of sin was. God had bruised him. He felt that God was his enemy, that God's wrath was upon him, and that he could not resist God or even stand before Him. The curse of God's law struck him down, and he lay bruised in the dust.

The reality of sin, and the astonishing nature of God's wrath, bruised him to such an extent that there was no healing. Now nothing can possibly comfort him unless he receives complete forgiveness and restoration. If there was the least doubt at this point, he could no longer rest. Was God's forgiveness a reality for him? He wanted to be assured of this by hearing God's voice of joy and gladness.

This is the reason why so many never come to the joy of God and never earnestly long for it. They have never truly felt the weight of their sins. They cannot speak to God of "the bones which Thou hast broken." They know that they are sinners, but the conviction is simply a thing of the understanding. The fear of the Lord is never upon them. They have never been moved by the sense of God's wrath. They do not feel that it is a terrible thing to fall into the hands of the living God. The spirit has not convinced them of sin. They have never learned to cry out, "Woe is me, I am undone." Therefore, they feel little need for joy and the certainty of God's forgiving love.

Lord, pour out your Holy Spirit so that many will know their sins and feel real anxiety in their soul. Let the law bruise them and the curse terrify them. Let the cross break them down so that they can find no rest until they find forgiveness and the joy of God in the blood of the cross.

Chapter 15

# YOUR SINS ARE HIDDEN

*"Hide Thy face from my sins"*—Psalm 51:9*a*.

"Hide thy face from my sins." David expresses in a new way what he wanted the grace of God to do for him. He expects God to hide His face from his sin and not see it anymore. This was also his aim in the prayer, "Have mercy upon me, O God."

## Our Sins Are Before God

This blessing is in total agreement with what the Word of God teaches us. As long as our sins are not forgiven, they stand before the face of God in order to accuse us. He hears the accusation which they bring against us. He looks at them in all their wickedness as a transgression of His law and they awake His anger and disapproval. God's Word says, "Thou hast set our iniquities before Thee, our secret sins in the light of Thy countenance" (Psalm 90:8). Also in Jeremiah 2:22 it says, "For though thou wash thee with nitre, and take thee much soap, yet thine iniquity is marked before Me, saith the Lord God."

In David's bitter experience this thought became a terrible truth. He feels not only what he confessed, "My sin is *ever before me,*" but what is more terrible, that his sin was *ever before God*. He saw his sins, and he was terrified. But, he also says that God saw them. Every sin he had committed was there before the face of God.

When you understand this fact, you will feel that every sin as soon as it is committed, goes to lengthen the list of your accusers before the face of God. Once a sin is committed, it is no longer in man's power. You cannot recall or annul it. No repentance, tears, or promise of new obedience can cover it or take it away. Only an act of God's free grace can give you the blessed certainty that your sin is no longer before God's face.

## Our Sins Are Hidden From God

What is this act of God? David calls it, "Hide Thy face from my sin." To hide the face from anything means not to see it. David's prayer is the same as what is said elsewhere in the Scriptures. For example in Numbers 23:21 it says, "He hath not beheld iniquity in Jacob, neither hath He seen perverseness in Israel." Hezekiah also prays: "But Thou hast in love to my soul delivered it from the pit of corruption: for Thou hast cast all my sins behind Thy back" (Isaiah 38:17). The prophet Micah also says, "He will turn again, he will have compassion upon us; he will subdue our iniquities; and Thou wilt cast all their sins into the depths of the sea" (Micah 7:19). In like manner the Lord speaks to the prophet Jeremiah. "In those days, and in that time, saith the Lord, the iniquity of Israel shall be sought for, and there shall be none. . .for I will pardon them whom I reserve" (Jeremiah 50:20). These words of Scripture help us to understand the forgiveness of God. He casts our sins behind His back. He throws them into the depths of the sea so that they can never be found. He turns His face from them and sees them no more.

This is blessedness, to know that our sins are forgiven. Christ has eliminated them. Our sins can no longer stand against us. The face of God that was turned away from our sins is now turned toward us in favor. God no longer sees our sin in anger. He looks at us in mercy. This is nothing different from what the New Testament calls justification. When the sinner is released from his sins, then he is a justified soul in the eyes of God. His former sins are no longer found. God has hidden His face from them. When the holy judge no longer sees them, then the acquitted soul can rejoice in the assurance of His favor and love.

At this point, however, someone may ask, How can the omniscient, faithful God, who knows my sin, shut His eyes to them and not notice them? He is always the Perfectly Righteous One. It is impossible for Him to look upon sin and notice it. When God turns His eyes from your sins, hides His face and casts your sins behind His back, He does this because satisfaction for them has been made through Jesus.

When He receives from Jesus the assurance that you belong to Him and have a part in the annulling of guilt by His blood, then God no longer has to deal with your sin. They have been put away. Then it is just His righteousness which demands that He should no longer remember your sins but hide His face from them. As long as your sins are before Him, God must look at them. But when they are charged to Jesus, with the satisfaction of Him as your payment, God cannot look at them anymore. They have been accounted for and discarded.

## Look To Jesus

We also learn in what spirit you are to make David's prayer your own, "Hide Thy face from my sins." Look at the Lord Jesus when He bore your sins to the cross and annulled the guilt of them. Look at Him with the complete atonement which He brought about and offered to you by God. Look at Him as given for you by God so that you can receive Him with confidence and come to God in Him.

Yes, look at Him as also waiting for you. Look at Him until your faith comes alive, and you can say, Jesus is also for me. God hides His face from my sins. "Thou hast cast all my sins behind Thy back."

This is a matter of great concern and amazing interest. All your sins are before the face of God. They cry out for vengeance. Day and night their cry ascends to God: "This sinner has angered You. He is worthy of the curse. O holy God, hide not Thy face from his sins." The law of God supports

84

their plea: "O holy God, they have transgressed Your law. Hide not Thy face from their sins." The sinner who must experience this is distressed. For this reason, let your prayer go up to God, "Hide Thy face from my sin." Plead the promise of God and the blood of Jesus. Ask Jesus to become your intercessor. You will see that God hears this prayer. The blood of Jesus has great power. He is in a position to cover your sins and to take them away from before God.

Chapter 16

# RECEIVING FORGIVENESS

*"And blot out all mine iniquities"*—Psalm 51:9*b*.

"And blot out all mine iniquities," this prayer is heard for the second time. It was the first word David used after he began to pray for mercy, in order to say what he wanted from it. He has already expressed his desires by other expressions, such as "Wash me"; "cleanse me"; "purge me"; "cause me to hear joy and gladness"; "hide Thy face from my sin." Once again he expresses them in these words, "Blot out all mine iniquities."

For an explanation of this statement, we refer to what has already been said in verse one. It is important for us to use this word to reflect on the preceding portion of the psalm. Also, this is the last time this point is referred to in the psalm. In the following three verses, David asks for an inward renewal of his heart by the Spirit of God. And, from verse 13 to the end of the psalm, he speaks of the fruits of the thanksgiving which God's redemption brings.

## Understanding Forgiveness

Before he proceeds David once again repeats the prayer, "Blot out all mine iniquities." In this way he shows us he was sincere about this matter. He knows that this is the root and beginning of all the rest. If there is no clear understanding between God and the sinner regarding the forgiveness of sins, there can be no further question about a new life. Therefore, friend, I will also deal with you on this matter earnestly, definitely, and with all sincerity. I want to ask you some questions concerning this all-important matter.

Do you thoroughly understand what the forgiveness of sins—*the blotting out of iniquities*—is? There are many earnest Christians who do not thoroughly understand that this is the foundation of our redemption. Do you understand that the blotting out of all sins is *the first blessing* God wants to give to the one who longs to be saved? Do you understand that God is prepared to give it immediately to everyone who receives it trustfully?

God offers it to us continually. Do you understand that if you sincerely take the Savior with His blood, you can receive it as a gift of God? Along with Jesus you actually receive, by faith, the blotting out of your sins. Do you know that by faith you can know that your sins are blotted out of God's Book? The Holy Spirit, as the Spirit of faith, bears witness to you of this forgiveness.

Do you understand that this blotting out is perfect and complete? Your soul appears before God "whiter than snow" and can look to God as a God who is no longer angry with you. Do you understand all this or is it still unclear to you? When we talk about these things, do you feel like someone who is still groping in the dark? See that you come to a clear understanding of these points, my friend, because your salvation depends on it.

## Seeking Forgiveness

Are you really seeking forgiveness and the blotting out of your sins? I am asking if you need to be saved, if you are restless, if you sometimes pray. Maybe you pray, "Forgive us our sins," every day. In the presence of God, the searcher of hearts, can you say that you are known to Him as one who really seeks for forgiveness? Can God declare that you are hungering and thirsting for it?

Can you say that day by day you are seeking and striving for this grace as something that is of vital importance? Have you given up sin and forsaken the world to obtain this forgiveness? And are you earnestly pleading before God to give you the one blessing which He has to give you?

Yes, are you really seeking it in church, in God's Word, in your prayer time, as the one thing for which you are willing to consider everything as loss? It is worth seeking after. God wants us to seek it. Only he who seeks it will obtain it. Are you really seeking it this way?

## Praying For Forgiveness

I have another question. If you have been seeking forgiveness, have you found it? Are your sins forgiven? Do you know that you are now clean in God's sight because He blotted out all your sins?

When David prayed for mercy, he was not content with indefinite ideas about the goodness of God. He knew what goodness wanted to do for him. He expected it to do something real for him. He prays for the blotting out of his sins with the hope of obtaining an answer to that prayer. He also prays in the hope that the joy and power of a new life will be fulfilled in him. So often he has sung of it in later psalms. For example, in Psalm 103:2,3 he says, "Bless the Lord, O my soul. . .who forgiveth all thine iniquities."

Therefore, I ask you, are your sins blotted out? If this is not the case, then you are not where you ought to be. You still do not have a part in God's salvation. I say to you, "Hurry to God." Do not remain standing far off. Believe. This blessing really can be found. This blessing is also for me. Sin can be destroyed.

Let your whole soul become fixed on this one aim—blotting out sin. Without this blessing there is no salvation. Only God can give it. He desires to give it. He will give it. God will perform this divine deed for you. He will take away all your sins. Just let this prayer be heard from the depths of your heart, "Blot out all mine iniquities." Let faith look on Christ. The Son of God can save sinners. He that believes in Him will not be ashamed.

Chapter 17

# CREATING A CLEAN HEART

*"Create in me a clean heart, O God"*—Psalm 51:10*a*.

In a preceding verse David had prayed, "Purge me with hyssop, and I shall be clean." We said that a man becomes clean when he is sprinkled with the blood of Jesus and is purged and set free from his sin. In this verse David again prays to be made clean, but the cleanness comes in another way. He prays that the Lord *create* within him a *clean* heart. He wants the Lord to make a new heart for him that is clean by His divine power.

David feels that there are two ways the unclean person can become clean before God. One is when he is washed and cleansed from his guilt in the blood of Jesus. He is judicially acquitted. The other happens when he is renewed, inwardly changed, and receives a new and clean heart in place of the old, unclean one. If you want to understand the way of salvation and the work of grace, strive to clearly understand this twofold purity.

## Pronounced Not Guilty

First, you must understand how the soul becomes acquitted by the blood of Jesus. By the acquittal and forgiveness of God a man is entirely freed from the guilt on him. Thus he is legally clean. That is to say, I have fulfilled the demands of the law. I have paid my guilt by myself or by another as my sacrifice. In that case, the law has nothing more to demand from me. I stand guiltless and clean. The law asks only about what I have done and what I have been. It does not ask what I still am or what I will do.

A judge on earth can acquit or pronounce clean without implying that the heart of the acquitted man is clean, or that he is beyond the possibility committing the very same sin again. In like manner, the sinner is acquitted and pronounced clean from all the sins he has committed, without it being implied that his heart is pure from the thought of future sins. Even though God knows the heart is inwardly impure as far as its sinful nature is concerned, the sinner is pronounced clean by the law as soon as all the demands of the law are fulfilled.

These demands have been fulfilled by the precious Savior's obedience and suffering. Therefore, the appropriation of Jesus has as its result the blessing of being pronounced clean in His blood. This is the purity David spoke of in the first half of the psalm. It is the complete forgiveness of sins, the being made "whiter than snow."

# Cleansing The Heart

But this purity is not all he needs. There is a second cleanness, the fruit and consequence of the first. An earthly judge can acquit a man or pronounce him clean even though his heart continues to hold on to his sins. He may leave the courtroom and commit them again. But God does not do this. He acquits the sinner and pronounces him clean only for Jesus' sake. He does not take into consideration the inward condition of his heart. He does not, however, leave him that way.

As soon as He acquits him, He begins the work of inward purification. The very same grace which teaches him to pray for the judicial cleansing from the acquittal of the law, also teaches him to desire the second purity, the inward cleansing that comes through the renewing of the Spirit. Therefore David, after he had prayed, "Purge me, and I shall be clean," "Wash me, and I shall be whiter than snow," again prays, "Create in me (inwardly also) a clean heart, O God." The one is as necessary as the other. The two are one. They are merely two different ways by which the purity of Jesus comes to man. As soon as a man believes, the righteousness of Christ is totally his, and he is welcome to God as one who is clean. The inward communication of the purity of Jesus to the soul takes place by degrees.

These two are one, but they should not be mixed together. This confusion takes place too frequently, and souls are lost. The one cleanness is a root, the other is a fruit. The one goes first, the other follows after. Pay particular attention to this. David has first prayed for the one (verse 7-9). Then he asks for the other. Never forget that the first, the cleansing of the blood of Christ, is granted before you can inwardly receive the second. Only if you receive and accept the first will you have the power to obtain the second.

Let this be your prayer, "Have mercy upon me, O God. Blot out my transgressions. Create in me a clean heart." Now we understand the place this prayer occupies in this psalm. It has better prepared us to feel its meaning and power. May God teach us to offer up this prayer earnestly and with our whole heart.

### Desire A Clean Heart

We must desire above all things to go on toward inward purity. David is not content simply praying for the forgiveness of his sins. No, he felt that his whole nature was inwardly corrupt. He also wants to be inwardly purified. He simply will not be content with acquittal from punishment. Unfortunately, many are quite content with this. No, he also wants to be free from the power and indwelling of sin. He feels that only according to the measure of his holiness can he enjoy God. "Blessed are the pure in heart: for they shall see God" (Matthew 5:8). Let this be your desire.

This clean heart must also be your expectation. God the Creator is also God the Renewer. He can do this. Just like the work of the first creation was completed step by step, so also will it be with the renewal. The holy God can perform this work. He can make the unclean heart clean. It is not too hard for Him. This is what grace will do for you. Let your expectation reach for this blessing. When you pray for forgiveness, let it be a step to becoming holy. God is pure, holy, and no prayer will be more welcomed by Him than that He make you holy also. "Create in me a clean heart, O God."

Chapter 18

# HAVING A STEADFAST SPIRIT

*"And renew a right (steadfast) spirit within me"*—Psalm 51:10*b* .

When God creates a clean heart, then man is born again. He is a new creature. He has received the new life, the love of God.

Nevertheless, it is not enough for a man to receive a new life. He must grow and be strengthened. A weak child is a living human creature and much has to be done for him to preserve, nourish, and lead that life until he becomes an adult. A weak child can stand and run, but he must also learn to stand fast. His behavior must also be established.

## The Importance Of Being Steadfast

This is what David prays for now. He not only wants a new life with a clean heart but also a *right* or a *steadfast* spirit. At the beginning that new life and purity of heart are weak and tender. Much has to be done to make it grow. The creation of God was not completed in one day. So also in the creation of a clean heart, time is needed before everything is finished, and man enters into his divine rest. After God has implanted the first principle of life in the new creation, man must willingly cooperate with God. He must with a right spirit surrender himself to the Lord and His work. The beginning of the new creation does not depend upon a steadfast spirit, but the progress of it does. The greater or less glory with which the creation shall be brought to completion also depends on it.

Great loss may be brought about by separating these two prayers from one another. They are inwardly bound up with one another. The person who is simply satisfied that he has received a new heart, does not persevere with a steadfast spirit to guard what he has received. If he does not try to use and increase what God has given him, the joy of the clean heart will become lost. On the other hand the one who works faithfully and prays for this right spirit, will have this purity of heart revealed within him. He will receive the full certainty and power of his heavenly birth.

We must also pray that God will give us *a steadfast spirit*. Steadfast is the opposite of weak, uncertain, changeable, variable. What stands fast cannot be moved or overthrown. Such a spirit must be asked from God in prayer. At the same time we must also observe in what ways God works and gives this blessing. This is the first thing that strikes us. *Faith is a sure foundation*. He who stands on it will not be moved. Therefore we read in Psalm 112:8 of the righteous man, "His heart is established, he shall not be afraid." Peter writes in 1 Peter 5:9, "steadfast in the faith." Paul also writes in Colossians 1:23, "If ye continue in the faith grounded and settled, and be not moved away from the hope of the gospel."

### Stand Fast On The Word Of God

In Hebrew the word "believe" comes from a word which means to be steadfast, to stand fast, and the word "believe" simply means to continue steadfast. Since God is a steadfast rock, the foundation of all certainty and reliability, man becomes steadfast by faith or clinging to God.

The more you hold on to God and commit yourself to His Word and counsel, the more faithful you will stand. If you want to know how God will give you this steadfast spirit, it is by the Word. Let the Word of God be your food. Inwardly absorb and appropriate it. Let it penetrate you and be flesh and blood to your spirit.

Strive to think what God thinks and will what God wills. In everything be of the same mind that God is. Grow by His Word and have it dwell in you. Then you will be established. In all your wishes, expectations, desires, and efforts, let what God has said be your rule, and a firm spirit will be renewed in you. If the Word of God is the rock of your confidence, you will not be moved, just like there is no variableness or shadow of turning with God.

How did Abraham become strong in faith in the

midst of so many severe trials? The root of his steadfastness was the promise of God. And why was it that Caleb and Joshua stood so firmly in the midst of the people of Israel? They held fast to the Word of God. And how did many other believers do it? The answer is simple. "They that trust in the Lord shall be as Mount Zion which cannot be removed, but abideth for ever"(Psalm 125:1). The spirit obtains its steadfastness and strength from God in His Word.

## A Steadfast Will

If you want to know how a steadfast spirit will manifest itself, the answer is not difficult. It is in the purpose of a steadfast will exercising dominion over the spirit and the walk. The great flaw in many believers who have a new heart is that they do not set themselves with a steadfast and resolute choice to cast out sin and do the will of God. They do not obey the orders of their conscience, the inward voice of the Spirit and the Word.

They do not surrender themselves to do the will of God as soon as they know it. There should be in every believer the holy purpose of doing the will of God without delay as soon as it is known. On this point I hope no uncertainty exists for there are many double-hearted souls who are unstable in all their ways. A divided heart makes them waver continually.

It is necessary to remember that along with a new heart and a sense of sin and good desire, there must also be a steadfast spirit which will be determined. It must set itself positively to fulfill all the commands of God. This steadfast spirit must be a matter of much prayer: "Renew a right (steadfast) spirit within me." At the same time it must strengthen our battle against sin. He who seeks it in prayer will certainly receive it and be able to join in David's song of deliverance in Psalm 40:2: "He brought me up also out of a horrible pit, Out of the miry clay, And set my feet upon a rock, And established my goings."

In the prayer for grace, in the life of grace, the steadfast spirit must have a place. The young tree not only must be planted, but must also become deeply rooted. Otherwise it can bear no fruit. Therefore let it be a continual prayer with you, "Make my footsteps steadfast in Thy Word, and let not any iniquity have dominion over me." Observe what the fruit of this prayer will be.

## Chapter 19

# LIVING IN GOD'S PRESENCE

*"Cast me not away from Thy presence"*—
Chapter 11*a*.

In his prayer, David proceeds to seek the blessings of the new life and also teaches us by the Holy Spirit what we may expect from grace. The clean heart and the steadfast spirit are great blessings. But, there is still something more which David desires—*the light of God's countenance*. He prays for the blessed experience of always walking in the presence of God as His friend.

## The Joy Of God's Presence

The promise of this blessing in the Word of God is very clear. It is frequently named as one of the privileges of God's children. For example in Psalm 89:15 it says, "Blessed is the people that know the joyful sound: They shall walk, O Lord, in the light of Thy countenance." It cannot be otherwise. What is the greatest joy of a child on earth? It is when his father or mother is pleased with him. We often see that the little child plays quietly and contentedly when he is with his mother in the room. The mother is busy and the child is busy. Just seeing his mother's face and knowing she is near is the joy of the child. God gives this privilege to those who receive from Him the name and the rights of children. In this world He always wants us to live before His face, in the light of His eyes, and with the assurance and experience of His love.

The value of this blessing is easily understood. What a heavenly joy it is to walk in the land of the living before the face of the Lord. What a joy it is to do all our work and carry on our conflict at the feet of our Father, knowing that "He looks down upon me with good pleasure." What a power it gives to be able to look up in every difficulty and in the middle of severe conflict and refresh myself with a glance at Him and be encouraged by His divine friendship. What a comfort it is in sorrow.

How can this blessing be enjoyed? The answer is not difficult. The child does not always need to be looking at his mother to enjoy being near her. The child is busy with his play or work, yet he immediately observes when his mother goes out. In the midst of all his work and play, he always has a hidden sense of her nearness. So it is with a true Christian. He can be so closely knit to his God that he cannot miss His presence. In the midst of all his activities on earth, there always remains the blessed feeling that "My God sees me, and I can look up to Him." He works under the eyes of God. Through this living and active faith, he beholds the invisible One and abides in His light. Just like one walks and works in the light on earth without always thinking about it, so there flows around him the spiritual experience of the presence of God as the light of his soul.

We must understand what a vital part this experience makes in our spiritual life. Do not forget that God's aim in His grace and your redemption is to restore the broken bond of fellowship and love between you and Him. True Christianity consists of the soul finding its highest happiness in personal communion with God.

Daily unbroken fellowship between God and you is what grace gives. Every day you must try to walk in the light of God's presence. If you want to know how to get to the point of living so that you can enjoy this blessing, this Psalm gives you the answer.

### How To Live In God's Presence

In the *first* place, be aware of the forgiveness of your sins. Hold on to the grace which has blotted out your guilt. Every day bring each new sin to the blood of Jesus so that you can be washed from it again. Every day seek a living certainty of the grace which sees you in righteousness of Jesus as being "whiter than snow." Look to the holy God who, for Jesus' sake, pronounced you righteous and loves you. Without this it will be impossible to walk in the light of God's presence. Remain secure in the faith that God is your God and your Father. Only by this faith can you continue in the enjoyment of the light and the love of God.

In the *second* place, strive to keep your heart pure. Let the passion of your soul burn strongly against all inward impurity and sin. Guard against negative or unholy attitudes. Remember, you must hate sin as God hates it. Keep in mind that you are redeemed to be holy, as God is holy. Let this be your fervent and earnest prayer, "A clean heart, O my God, a clean heart." Knowing that the work of the new creation is not finished at once, ask God to accomplish His work in you. A redeemed soul who remains content with what he has and does not earnestly desire to be holy, cannot walk in the light of God's presence. His worldly thinking and his carnal attitudes are a cloud which separate him from God.

In the *third* place, maintain a steadfast spirit. You must have a steadfast determination of the heart, a firm choice of a strong will to walk in God's presence. While you hold on to forgiveness and desire purity of heart, determine not to rest until you have experienced the blessing of always abiding in the pleasure of God's presence.

Begin every morning with this steadfast purpose and seal it with believing prayer that God will keep you from everything that might turn you away from His presence. Let this be your will because it is also the will of God, then you will obtain the blessing. You will find that grace will do this for you. God will hear your prayer, "Cast me not away from Thy presence." In this blessed experience you will be able to say with joy, "Oh, how great is Thy goodness, which Thou hast wrought for them that trust in Thee before the sons of men! Thou shalt hide them secretly in a pavilion from the strife of tongues. Blessed be the Lord: for He hath shewed me His marvelous kindness in a strong city" (Psalm 31:19-21).

## Chapter 20

## ASKING FOR THE HOLY SPIRIT

*"And take not Thy Holy Spirit from me"*—
Psalm 11*b*.

David has sought a great blessing, a very gracious gift from God. He asks that he may always walk before His presence and in the light of it. He has asked that his whole life be illumined by the immediate presence of God, living under His eye, and in His favor. David wants his whole life on earth to be spent in conversation with His God in heaven. Grace is prepared to give us this glorious life.

Walking on earth in fellowship with God in heaven is a wonderful experience. But, that the Most High would come down from His heaven *to dwell in my heart* and consecrate it to be His temple—certainly this is the full glory of what grace has destined for us. This is what David craves in the prayer, "Take not Thy Holy Spirit from me." He yearns for the conscious indwelling of the Holy Spirit.

## The First Work Of The Spirit

Some may think that this petition is not in the proper place. Nothing is ever worked in us except by the Spirit. Even the first conviction of sin and the desire to pray for grace must come from Him. Should prayer for the Spirit, then, *precede* everything else? The answer to this question should be given several considerations.

The working of the Holy Spirit in a sinner who desires salvation is indeed essential, but it is a hidden and unconscious desire. He does not know that the anxiety arising from the conviction of sin and his earnest pleas for mercy are the results of the Spirit's operations. On the other hand, when at a later time he does accept the Lord, he has the promise that he will know the Spirit. The Spirit will not only work in him but will establish His presence in him so that he will know and feel it.

This, for example, is the promise given to those who were baptized on the day of Pentecost. They had already, at the outset, experienced the operation of the Spirit. "Repent. . . and ye shall receive the gift of the Holy Ghost"(Acts 2:38). The Lord Himself said to His disciples after they had experienced the first workings of the Spirit, "If ye love Me, keep My commandments. And I will pray the Father, and He shall give you another Comforter"(John 14:15,16).

### The Believer's Pledge

David's prayer here is not a petition for the first

operation of the Spirit which is conversion. Such prayer is necessary, according to the will of God, and must be prayed. But the petition here in Psalm 51 asks for that indwelling of the Spirit of God which is the privilege of the believer. The Spirit dwells in us to teach us (see John 16:13,14), to seal us and give us the assurance of sonship (see Romans 8:15,16). The Spirit comes to sanctify and prepare us for heaven (see Romans 8:11).

This is the lesson, taught to the believer in this petition. We can expect not only a clean heart, a steadfast spirit, the light of God's face, but *also* the indwelling of God's Spirit in our heart. Every believer may have and ought to experience this blessing. Without this he does not live according to the will of God.

David's prayer makes this clear. "Take not Thy Holy Spirit from me." He speaks as one who has already received the Holy Spirit. David asks that the Spirit not be taken from him. He feels that, although his former great sin has been forgiven, he still runs the risk of grieving and quenching the Holy Spirit. The Holy Spirit is the Spirit of grace who strives with sinners, but He is still the Holy Spirit who can be driven away by the love of sin.

David knows that our worldly ways, our fears, and our lack of attention to His workings, can injure the Spirit. He is grieved and He withdraws His presence from us. This also happens when we are unfaithful in the use of the Word and prayer, on which His work depends. It is with the sense of this great danger of grieving the Spirit that David prays, "Take not Thy Holy Spirit from me."

This petition is part of the prayer for grace. It is only due to the grace of God if the Holy Spirit is not taken away from believers. As often as injury is done to Him, He is dishonored and has reason to withdraw. Were He not the Spirit of grace, He would certainly leave us. David hoped and begged that the Spirit of God would not withdraw from him, even when he deserved to be left alone.

## Lessons For The Believer

There are two lessons the believer can learn from David's prayer.

*First,* the *Holy Spirit will dwell in the believer*. If you desire to be led in the way of grace by the hand of David you must keep yourself occupied with the promise of the Spirit. You must search in the Word of God for all the promises concerning the operation of the Spirit. You must know that this gift is presented to you. You must yield yourself completely to the Lord to experience this glorious grace. You must seek to live daily in the fellowship of the Spirit. You will discover that this is the highest blessing that can be experienced on earth.

In the *second* place, the *blessing of the Holy Spirit must be a distinct request* in the prayer for grace. The person who wants salvation must feel that he is unworthy of this blessing. Every day he must realize that God does him a favor by not taking away His Spirit. According to the sincerity of his desire, prayer, and faith, his growth in the

Holy Spirit will take place. His communion with the Spirit will become more effective and realistic.

The neglect of David's prayer will result not only in the loss of this blessing but also in the suppression of other blessings that have previously been enjoyed. Therefore, we should pray with all sincerity, "Take not Thy Holy Spirit from me."

Chapter 21

# THE JOY OF SALVATION

*"Restore unto me the joy of Thy salvation"*—
Psalm 51:12*a*.

We have seen earlier that David spoke of a twofold cleansing. First, there was a judicial cleansing that resulted in freedom from guilt. It is the fruit of the divine acquittal on the basis of the atonement of Christ, "the being washed in the blood of Christ." Also, there was an inward cleansing worked out by the creative, renewing energy of the Holy Spirit.

David also speaks of a twofold joy, as seen in his psalm. Previously he said, "Make me to hear joy and gladness"(verse 8). This word stands between the repeated petition for forgiveness (verses 1-9), and relates this first joy to forgiveness of sins. The prayer which we have here in verse 12, teaches us that the joy of God's salvation is not only the desire of those just converted. It is equally destined for the Christian who is striving on the pathway of growth and sanctification.

# Joy And Forgiveness

Let us think carefully about this connection. We have already seen that the first joy of the person who received salvation depends on the knowledge of forgiveness. The sinner becomes aware of his sin and cannot possibly rejoice in God, unless he knows God as the One who has blotted out his sin. He knows that if he has not received this blessing, God is still his enemy and a consuming fire. Only when the soul comes to the cross and receives an interest in the atonement of Christ can the thought of the holy God fill him with gladness. It is fellowship with the reconciling God that brings joy.

In like manner, the continuance and growth of the soul's joy depends on deepening communion with God. The very first act of God, the forgiveness of sins, begins this fellowship with the soul, and imparts gladness. God's next work in the soul is sanctification. Through His work of restoration, He establishes in it the clean heart and the steadfast spirit, a life in the light of His presence, and the indwelling of the Holy Spirit. This also brings much joy.

Just as the soul cannot experience its first gladness without forgiveness, it cannot experience continued joy apart from a holy life. Just as the guilt of old sin robs the soul of joy until it knows it is forgiven, new sin that is not confessed fills the soul with darkness.

The joy of forgiveness will not always remain unless it is confirmed as the joy of sanctification.

In this experience many Christians have had heavy losses, through lack of carefulness or knowledge. When the first joy began to disappear, he did not know the cause or else he was unfaithful in not confessing the sad fact to God. He attributed the loss to God as a trial which He had sent him.

If he had only asked for grace, to be washed from guilt and be freed from the dominion of sin. Then he would have discovered that with the progressive work of grace in the soul a progressive joy would have been ministered to him by God. It is the joy of God's *salvation* for which David prays. There is joy in God's salvation. As we yield ourselves to God for it, we will enjoy it.

So this twofold joy is one. We have already discussed this concerning the twofold purity. It is also true with the joy. It is sin that causes pain and misery. It is becoming free from sin that brings light and gladness. It is one God who rolls away the curse and guilt of sin in one moment, and then gradually makes the soul free from its power. The joy is also one.

## Joy And Holiness

The person who rejoices in forgiveness ought to know that there is joy, that is still sweeter, deeper, and more glorious than this. It takes place when the freedom from sin and fellowship with God are applied to living a holy life. The joy of forgiveness is the beginning for the newly-born child of God. It is the milk of the blessing. The joy of sanctification and fellowship with God is for those who have grown up. It is the solid food, the ripe fruit of joy.

Let this petition sink deep into your heart. The joy and blessedness of God are His perfect holiness. The joy of His children is also the joy of holiness. Without a clean heart and a holy walk the Christian cannot continuously experience joy.

The life of sanctification is joy. The way of a clean heart under the leading of the Spirit, was once seen as a grevious way filled with groans and fears. God has changed it into a way of joy. At first, some sacrifice of the flesh may appear unwelcome and severe. But God has said that if you yield yourself to living a holy life, you will find great reward and the joy of His salvation in His service.

It is only as the salvation of God is actually experienced that joy can be tasted. Joy is not a separate gift which can be received and enjoyed apart from further experience of God's salvation. It is the joy *of that salvation* and it is tasted as you surrender yourself to that salvation and the redeeming, sanctifying grace of God who gives it. There are so many Christians who seek the comfort and joy of redemption, and even pray for it, yet do not find it.

Others who are less anxious about joy and concentrate on seeing and tasting the salvation of God, and doing all that He requires, are glad in the Lord and filled with the joy of His salvation. If you want to be glad, simply cling to the Lord, the source of all joy. If you want joy, surrender to the salvation of the Lord. First in the assurance of forgiveness, then in devotion to living a holy life. Then, with confidence, ask and expect "a joy that is unspeakable and full of glory."

Chapter 22

## LIVING IN FREEDOM

*"And uphold me with Thy free spirit"*—Psalm 51:12*b*.

Grace restores man to a right relationship with God. It also restores him to a right relationship to himself. As a result of this, he comes to have right attitudes toward his fellow-men. When grace makes the soul part of the favor of God and the Spirit of God, the joy of God's salvation is shed abroad in the heart. As the fruit of this blessing, heart and mouth are opened to make others acquainted with the grace of God. It is this blessing that David now asks for from the divine mercy. He feels his calling, and he is aware of his weakness. In the midst of these feelings, he asks for help from above.

### Being A Living Witness

David *realizes his calling.* Every believer must be a witness and an example of the grace of God. He is obligated, for the honor of God and the salvation of others, to tell what great things the

116

Lord has done for him. He knows that the living witness is better than dead legalism. Only when believers confess with boldness what God has done for them will the world be forced to acknowledge the work of God and adore His grace. Only by their speech and lifestyle can they prove that God is faithful.

In the world they must give convincing proof of what grace can really do. A candle is never lit among men to be hid under a bushel. The eternal God wants His people, the light of the world, to let their light shine. David knew all this. Just as he confessed his sin and asked for redemption, he also prepares himself for the service of thanksgiving and of love.

David is also *aware of his own weakness*. The feeling which he expresses in Psalm 116:10, "I believed, therefore have I spoken," was the expression of his own experience. He knew that unless he had the Spirit of faith he could not know how to speak correctly. He realized that there was still in him the fear of man, as well as his own laziness and unfaithfulness. Therefore, it was important to him to pour out a prayer for this gift of divine grace, "Uphold me with Thy free spirit."

### Grace To Be A Witness

David knew he could count on the grace of God to give him this blessing. Grace is prepared to put the soul in a position to praise God and confess His name in the midst of every duty to which it is called. This is a point that believers do not understand. They feel that the forgiveness of sin is an act of mere grace on the part of God. They acknowledge that the sanctification of a life must also be worked out by grace. They do not know that the free spirit, with its power, must also be the gift of free grace. They think that openly confessing the grace of God and proclaiming His goodness to others is the work they are expected to do for the Lord out of gratitude. But, they do not feel adequate for this duty and remain helpless in their weakness and unfaithfulness, full of guilt and failure.

Some people are not aware that grace not only begins the work of redemption but also completes it. With the same certainty that they first prayed for forgiveness, they can also expect God to put them in a position to fulfill their vows of thanksgiving. It was with confidence that David prayed, "Have mercy upon me. Uphold me with a free spirit."

## Freedom To Be A Witness

The words "a free spirit" are very important. "Where the Spirit of the Lord is, there is liberty" (2 Corinthians 3:17). There is freedom from all oppression, fear and doubt that can weaken the soul. Only a complete surrender of the heart to be filled by the Spirit will bring freedom. It is only freedom before God that makes us free in our relationships to people. To have this full confidence before God, it is necessary that we look to Him, fellowship with Him, and be conscious of being

118

surrendered to His will and service. The person who has this assurance in his heart before God never needs to fear any man. The continued awareness of God's friendship, nourished in fellowship with Him, will make us free from the dominion of the fear of man. And, it will put us in a position to testify and praise God freely.

Believer, pray for a free spirit. Grace will certainly give it to you. You hinder the work of grace in your life if you remain without this blessing. You are content with half of what the grace of God is prepared to do for you. You defraud grace of the honor due to it, if you remain satisfied without this gift. It is yours. It is your privilege to walk with a free spirit in the face of the world and sin, as a child of the heavenly King. Live the life of grace. Receive the blessings of redemption as they are presented in the verses of this psalm. Let the joy of God's salvation fill you. In answer to prayer this free spirit will also become your most cherished possession. If you do not have it, let your faith stretch out and expect it in sincere, earnest prayer. "Uphold me with a free spirit." Out of the riches of the grace of God, you will certainly obtain it.

## Chapter 23

## TELLING OTHERS ABOUT JESUS

*"Then will I teach transgressors Thy ways"*—
Psalm 51:13*a*.

The third part of this Psalm begins here. The first part dealt with confession of sin. After this came prayer for the redemption David desired—forgiveness of sin and renewal of the heart by the Spirit of God. Now comes the fruit of redemption. He will praise the Lord and make His grace known to others. As a servant of God, he will submit himself to the great work of teaching sinners God's ways.

### God's Purpose For You

This is the goal of God with every person to whom He makes His grace known. For all God's children this word holds true, "This people have I formed for Myself; they shall shew forth My praise" (Isaiah 43:21). This agrees with the language of Paul, "Howbeit for this cause I obtained mercy, that in me first Jesus Christ might shew forth all longsuffering, for a pattern to them which should hereafter believe on Him to life everlasting" (1 Timothy 1:16). God must have honor from his work, and this honor is given to Him when a ransomed soul praises Him and speaks about the great things He has done for him.

On earth no one lights a candle and puts it under a bushel. Neither would the Most High God of heaven do it. To everyone He brings out of the kingdom of darkness He says, "Ye are the light of the world" (Matthew 5:14). "Let your light shine" (Matthew 5:16). If you have offered up this prayer for grace to teach others, then fix your attention on what the Holy Spirit can teach you from David's prayer. The design of grace is to make you a witness for the love of God, and a monument of His wonderful goodness. Surrender yourself to this aim and plan of God. Say in His strength when you pray for grace, "Then will I teach transgressors Thy ways."

## Motivated By Love

God does not require this teaching as a debt you must pay in return for your redemption. If you will yield yourself to this work in the strength of grace, it will be your greatest joy to say, "Then will I teach transgressors Thy ways." When you think of the pit out of which you have been rescued and the glorious salvation that is yours, your heart will be filled with compassion for sinners. When you think of the deep misery of others and how God's precious grace is ready to redeem them as it has redeemed you, you will consider it a blessing to exercise the privilege of speaking to them about Jesus.

When you think about what the love of Jesus has done for you, and how much you have to thank Him for, this love will motivate you. As often as you pray, "O God, have mercy upon me, then will I teach transgressors Thy ways," the desire will be awakened in you for others to know Him as you know Him. You can be sure that only then will they be truly happy. Then they also will glorify the Lord. You feel more than you can express in words, how worthy He is to be known and glorified.

### The Joy Of Telling Others

The thought that a "transgressor" might be awakened to life, that this worldly person might be changed into an example of the grace of God— through your prayer and teaching—is enough to make your heart burst with joy. And this will not seem impossible if you look to Him to make use of your service.

You probably think you are unprepared for this task. You do not know how you will ever be in a position to teach sinners God's ways. The joy and gladness of redemption are almost taken away from you for fear of having to face this awesome duty. Observe that this promise results from a prayer for grace. David merely says that, if God shows him favor, restores to him the joy of His salvation, and grants him the upholding of a free spirit, then he will teach transgressors His ways.

*The Lord does not require more of you than what He Himself will enable you to perform.*

To a person who has had his heart filled with grace, it is a joy and pleasure to make others acquainted with Jesus. The reason it is so difficult to speak about Jesus is that we are content with so little of the grace of God. We do not yield ourselves to be completely filled with it. Let the fear you feel convince you that you do not yet have as much grace as God is prepared to give. God will gladly give every soul so much blessing that his mouth will overflow because his heart is full. He will not be able to remain silent. Love for Jesus and for others will force him to speak.

Go to God more earnestly, with prayer for the full joy of the forgiveness of sins and for the full indwelling of the Spirit. Then, you will also teach transgressors His ways. This is what God desires from those who have been enriched with His grace. It is through this service that you will discover true joy and the full power of grace. You ask where, when, to whom, and how are you to teach God's ways. The Lord will make all this known to you. The compulsion of love will teach you this. Love will seek and create opportunities. Are you ill? You still have a grand opportunity to teach others. Is your circle of friends narrow and limited? In your own house there may be someone who does not know God's ways. Are you simple and uneducated? The plain words of an ordinary person often find the fullest entrance into the hearts of others.

The world is full of transgressors, and the heart of Jesus is full of love. If you have really tasted His love, you must admit that the most glorious work is being the messenger of this love to redeem those who are going to hell. This grace which made you born again is also able to open your mouth to speak this wonderful blessing to others. Every person who has been given grace is called to the work of teaching sinners God's ways. You will receive strength to carry it out with a willing, joyful heart.

## Chapter 24

# BEING USED BY GOD

*"And sinners shall be converted unto Thee"*—
Psalm 51:13*b*.

We have seen how deeply David felt about his sin. If there was anyone who had reason to be ashamed, never to trust himself, and to be silent, it was David. If there was anyone who had reason to say he did not know what might happen to him, it was David. If there was anyone who, because of his unfaithfulness, had reason to say that he had no right to speak, it was David. No one was under an obligation to listen to him. Because of his sin, his words would have little impact. How exalted David had been in other days, and how deeply he had fallen.

In this Psalm, David is in conversation with God and His grace. In his prayer, he already anticipates the glory of God's grace. He feels that the grace of God is more powerful than his sin. Since grace could take away his sin before God, it could also give him access to men. He feels that if grace redeemed him, the chief of sinners, and showed its great goodness to him, it would also be prepared to make use of him as a blessing to others. Therefore he not only promises, "I will teach transgressors Thy ways," but also believes that God will certainly bless his work. "Sinners shall be converted unto Thee." He trusts in grace for others as he does for himself. The grace which has blessed him will make him a blessing. "I will teach transgressors Thy ways; *and sinners* shall be converted unto Thee."

There is power in the confidence that there will be blessing on our work. A person can work with enthusiasm and pleasure when he knows that God will give the increase. How can we increase this confidence? Let us carefully consider the source of our confidence.

## Confidence In God

First of all, remember that conversion occurs when certain things are done. *"I will* teach transgressors; sinners shall be converted." It is not enough to mourn over the poor unbelieving world. It is not even enough to pray for the conversion of sinners. Something more is needed. *They must be taught.* This teaching should not just be done on the Lord's day or handed over to preachers of the gospel. Every believer must within his own circle of friends faithfully perform and carry out the promise. After praying, "Have mercy upon me," the promise must follow, "I will teach." God is faithful to bring about conversion. What a marvelous change would take place in our churches if every believer would become a witness for God. Faithful witnessing would encourage the expectation that "sinners will be converted unto Thee."

Observe, in what spirit we are to witness. David says that, as one who is pardoned, and has received forgiveness from God and the joy of His salvation, he will teach transgressors. How many preachers, Sunday school teachers, Christian elders, and friends there are whose teaching has no power. They never see the fulfilment of the hope: "Sinners shall be converted unto Thee." It is not from lack of teaching the truth, but from failing to speak about a living experience of this grace. They teach from a knowledge of the truths of Scripture or refer to an earlier spiritual experience. But, this is not enough. If you want to see teaching and conversion of sinners, you must have a living, effective experience of the grace of God. Blotting out your guilt in a daily use of the blood of Jesus must be the joy of your soul.

Your Christian walk must be carried out by purifying your heart and renewing a steadfast spirit in your inner being. With the prayer, "Take not Thy Holy Spirit from me," your whole being must be one where Jesus lives in your heart. With the sincere petition, "Uphold me with a free spirit," this purpose must be renewed continually and acted on, "I will teach transgressors Thy ways."

This must be your effort and your prayer. When you say with the desire of this psalm, "Then will I teach," you may also add, "sinners shall be converted unto Thee." Let your teaching of others be the fruit of His indwelling grace. Then, it cannot remain unblessed. Daily wash in the blood of Jesus and seek the anointing of His Spirit. Live near to Jesus, and "sinners shall be converted."

## Confidence In Prayer

Observe that this confidence must be nourished and expressed in prayer. David did not look to himself and his power. It was while he looked to God in prayer that David spoke those glorious words of faith. Speak this prayer on your knees with your eye fixed on God who has shown you His grace. This hope is not too much to expect, "I will teach, and sinners shall be converted." If at the beginning you do not succeed in using these words in full faith, then say the prayer again. Express the hope again to Him who sits on the throne of grace.

Begin with the first starting point, "Have mercy upon me, O God," and climb this ladder of prayer by the various steps of the spiritual life. Make sure of each stage in your own heart until you come to this, "I will teach transgressors." Then the Spirit of prayer, who has taught you to use all the other petitions, will enable you to speak this word with increasing confidence, *"sinners shall be converted unto Thee."* Just as prayer and conflict became the power that led you to speak this word, so will it become your power to say to sinners,

"Sinners shall be converted; I will teach transgressors."

"Have mercy upon me, O God. Then will I teach transgressors; and sinners shall be converted unto Thee."

## Chapter 25

# DELIVERED FROM GUILT

*"Deliver me from bloodguiltiness, O God, Thou God of my salvation"*—Psalm 51:14a.

David has made a great promise. He is to teach transgressors God's ways. At the same time, he has expressed his expectation that by his teaching sinners will be converted. The words are scarcely out of his lips when he again feels how sinful he is, and how it can only be through supernatural grace that such a result will ever be achieved. He feels that Uriah's blood has defiled him in the presence of God and man. If God gives him the perfect, living assurance that he is fully acquitted from his sins, then he will be able to praise God in truth.

## A Daily Reality

The living personal experience of grace is necessary if we are to tell others about Jesus. A person must not waver in the enjoyment of his own redemption. The memory of forgiveness and grace experienced at an earlier stage is not enough. Every day there must be a renewal of the divine assurance that we are redeemed by God. There must be a living reality of salvation as a present fact, a continually renewed and fresh exercise of fellowship with the God of redemption. The person who does not know God in this way cannot make Him known to others. David felt this. How could he, the murderer of Uriah, stained with the guilt of blood, bring life to others while he must still give an account of the blood of Uriah?

It is impossible for me to teach others, if I do not know God correctly myself. And man does not know God correctly if he does not know Him as the God of forgiveness. Moreover, this knowledge cannot be living and real if it is not continually renewed from heaven by the Holy Spirit. Every time that I give my testimony, to teach sinners so that they will be converted, it must be with the prayer, "Deliver me, O God, Thou God of my salvation: and my tongue shall sing aloud of Thy righteousness."

## The Guilt Of Sin

When one considers the words of this petition closely, these thoughts will be more fully confirmed. Let us think about the word that is used here in this prayer. *Deliver* me from bloodguiltiness. This is a term that we have not seen in this psalm. It is commonly used, not so much of setting free from sin, as of deliverance from enemies that pursue and oppress us. An example of this is the prayer, "Deliver us from evil" (Matthew 6:13).It is from this point of view that David now

131

contemplates his sins. He believes that God has forgiven them. He is also assured that he has been washed from them.

Sometimes there are occasions in a believer's life when sins that have been forgiven, rise up again and pursue and overtake the soul. God has forgiven them, but the person who committed them cannot forget them. He is afraid there will be a new outbreak of their evil. The great enemy, Satan, makes use of these times of oppression to utterly cast our souls down to the dust. In that case there is only one remedy. God alone can deliver us from the heavy burden of guilt.

But He *can* do it. He can give us such a view of the completeness of His forgiveness and grace, that we will be delivered out of the hand of our enemies and know that sin will have no more dominion over us. He can make us understand the full significance of the glorious words of the New Testament, "He was manifested to take away our sins" (1 John 3:5) in order that we may have "no more conscience of sins" (Hebrews 10:2). Through the Holy Spirit, God fully reveals to us the redemption of the Lord Jesus, so that we have the full answer to the petition, "Deliver me from bloodguiltiness, O God, Thou God of my salvation."

The enjoyment of such complete deliverance becomes the urgent desire to sing of His righteousness. If you do not know if you can celebrate God's praise, come and experience this blessing. Let it become a matter of living knowledge in your heart how glorious it is to be delivered by God. Then your mouth will sing the praise of this God.

## Personal Salvation

This same idea is found in the very name by which David designates God, "O God, Thou God of my salvation." It is because he is the God of *my salvation* that I joyfully want to praise Him. The personal relationship between God and men and the living assurance and experience of it are essential for this to take place. At the same time this experience empowers me to make Him known. If you want to know how to succeed in calling God by this name, learn from David's example.

In the beginning of this psalm, David was not prepared to use the proper word. He several times addressed the Lord as "God," but not as "my God." Under the power of continued prayer, as well as the constantly renewed plea for grace, his faith is strengthened. The Spirit of God has given him courage to hold fast to God. "Thou art the God of my salvation." It is also the same with you. If with every sin, old or new, you cast yourself before Him pleading for the fullness of His grace—forgiveness, renewal, and complete redemption—you will be given courage in the midst of such prayer to say with all the spiritual freedom of faith, "The God of *my salvation*." May all who are looking for this assurance of faith come to a full understanding of this fact. It is not a matter for argument, but it is learned in prayer.

The one who wants to truly say to Him, "Thou art my God, the God of my salvation," must obtain the privilege in prayer.

When a person has learned to use this language of faith toward God, it will not be so difficult to use it toward men. It is impossible to speak freely with God and yet hesitate to speak with people. As we speak to God in secret, we must confess Him in public. The principal characteristic of the good news to others is the confession, He is the God of *my* salvation. What He has done for me, He can also do for you. I speak from experience. What the Word says, I confirm with all the certainty of personal knowledge. The God who has redeemed me will also redeem you.

## Chapter 26

# THE MEANING OF RIGHTEOUSNESS

*"And my tongue shall sing aloud of Thy righteousness"*—Psalm 51:14 *b*.

After the petition, comes the promise. Grace does not selfishly desire personal enjoyment or safety, but gives itself to honor God and bless others. David's experience of fellowship with God, as the God of his salvation, causes him to praise God. "Deliver me from bloodguiltiness, O God, Thou God of my salvation; and my tongue shall sing aloud of Thy righteousness."

The words of this promise are very significant and instructive. First of all, observe the main theme of this joyful celebration. It is the righteousness of God. It is as if this psalm of grace and redemption could not end without this word in which the work of God in connection with our redemption is presented. The Holy Spirit uses *the righteousness of God* to indicate to us the origin, way, and fruit of our redemption.

# The Righteousness Of God

Righteousness embraces in one word an attribute of God, the gift with which we are endued, and the operation of this redemption in our life. For the person who wants to be saved or for those who have been recently converted, the word *grace* has a beautiful sound and appears to be most attractive and encouraging. The growing knowledge of grace will always bring us to the righteousness of God where the love of God has its foundation and the believer seeks his stability. Therefore, to the first promise to teach transgressors God's ways, these words are added: the resolve to proclaim His righteousness. Let us try to understand this word.

*First* of all, righteousness indicates the attribute of God that moves and guides Him in the giving of grace. Grace in the forgiveness of our unrighteousness is not exhibited at the expense of the righteousness of God. Grace reigns through righteousness. It is from the righteousness of God that grace receives its power. So John writes, "If we confess our sins, He is faithful and just (or righteous) to forgive us our sins" (1 John 1:9). Paul also says that God is righteous when He justifies the ungodly (Romans 3:26; 4:5). In the psalms and prophets, this righteousness of God is frequently mentioned as that which His people especially celebrate and rejoice.

Some have not been able to understand this and

think that in these passages the word righteousness must be synonymous with goodness. This is not the case. The righteousness of God, His character which always does what is right, is the foundation of His throne of grace. Believers understand that the only way the unrighteous can be redeemed and become righteous is that God, the only righteous One, will communicate His righteousness to them.

## The Righteousness Of Christ

The phrase, "Thy righteousness," further means the righteousness that is given to the sinner in God's gracious sentence of acquittal. David had prayed, "Wash me, and I shall be whiter than snow." That "whiter than snow" can be maintained only in the possession of the righteousness of God. The New Testament makes it plain how this can be. The righteousness of God is brought to us by the Mediator, the man Christ Jesus. By His obedience and suffering Jesus has brought us an everlasting righteousness.

Just as by the sin of the first Adam death reigned over all that belong to him, so through the righteousness of the second Adam grace comes to all who cling to Him. Faith is reckoned as righteousness to Abraham and through all succeeding periods of Israel's history. It is the grace of God which justifies the ungodly, and that has been the hope and joy of His people. "In the Lord shall all the seed of Israel be justified, and shall glory" (Isaiah 45:25).

## The Joy Of Righteousness

Then, this word also signifies the effect of the grace of God. The sentence of acquittal by which God justifies the sinner and the righteousness of Christ which he obtains become power for sanctification. They are are in him the seed of a new life of righteousness. "He that doeth righteousness is righteous, even as He is righteous" (1 John 3:7). Grace reigns through righteousness *unto life*. Grace renews the soul after the likeness and spirit of the Righteous One. The righteousness of God in Christ, first assigned by faith, becomes the new nature in which God's children walk. "If ye know that He is righteous, ye know that every one that doeth righteousness is born of Him" (1 John 2:29).

According to the New Testament the full significance of this word is "the righteousness of God." And, this is just what David said, "My tongue shall sing aloud of Thy righteousness." The revelation of it was so delightful and worthy of admiration that David not only wanted to speak of it but also to celebrate its value and worth. He gloried in it as something that had now become his. *Joyfully* he praised God for it. This was not a burden on him, a mere fulfillment of duty, but something that was his delight. He spoke of it with joy and gladness.

On every occasion, draw near to God for a new experience of the righteous grace of the Lord in complete deliverance from your guilt. Then you will joyfully celebrate the righteousness of the

Lord. Every repetition of the prayer, "Deliver me, O God, Thou God of my salvation," will give you strength and joy for the promise, "And my tongue shall sing aloud of Thy righteousness."

## Chapter 27

## SPEAKING FORTH HIS PRAISES

*"O Lord, open Thou my lips; and my mouth shall shew forth Thy praise"* —Psalm 51:15.

The promise to praise God is repeated again. It is preceeded, however, by the prayer that grace will give the strength to fulfill it. We have already seen that the full, living experience of God's salvation will agree to praise God. On the other hand, this worship without the experience is an impossibility. Furthermore, it is a gift asked in prayer and then obtained.

### Excuses For Silence

This petition reminds us of the natural reluctance and inability of man to speak of God and to witness of His grace. Every believer's experience confirms this truth. We keep silent even when we enjoy the grace of God and eagerly desire to work for Him. Sometimes it is our fear of mockery and contempt from others. At other times it is unbelief, or a feeling of being unprepared that takes away all courage and delight in witnessing. There is also that hidden self-centeredness that finds an excuse in its own spiritual need. Another excuse is humility which is afraid of injuring God's name by confessing Him now and then becoming disloyal and unfaithful later. Many believers could tell of a time when they wanted to work for the Lord. They could tell of the months and years they spent wishing and longing until their silence became a habit and their conscience, by all sorts of excuses, became passive.

If they had only understood what the difference is between sinful silence and impetuous speech. If they had only understood that, along with the forgiveness of sins and the renewal of the life, *grace will also give the ability to speak*. The continued prayer, "Have mercy upon me, O God, open my lips," will be heard.

## The Lord Help Us Speak

This prayer recorded here by the Spirit of God assures us that the Lord can and will open the lips. The one who sincerely desires to believe this simply has to reflect on what is recorded in the Word of God. Read the history of Moses. Let the wonderful arguments by which God showed him His power to give him a speaking mouth, sink deep into your soul (Exodus 4:10-12). Everyone who will humbly listen to these divine words of encouragement will be strengthened in this confidence.

Also, read the story of the calling of Jeremiah (Jeremiah 1:7-9) and the other prophets. See how fully He presents the power to speak as one of His gifts. Consider the promises of the Old Testament about the gift of the Spirit and observe how it is accompanied by the power to speak. Notice the predictions of Jesus concerning witnessing for Him as the fruit of the gift of the Spirit (John 15:26,27; Acts 1:8). Remember on the day of Pentecost the first manifestation of the power of the exalted Christ was to fill the mouth of the disciples with God's praise.

A high calling and divine certainty is attached to the opening of the lips as a gift of grace. It truly belongs to us. *God can give it*. He has done it for thousands. *God will give it*. It is necessary for the accomplishment of His glorious work of grace. *God shall give it*. His promises are faithful. "Lord, open my lips." We have as much right to this prayer as the other, "Have mercy upon me, O God." The one is heard as certainly as the other.

## The Gift Of Speaking

David's prayer teaches us the way to obtain this gift. Whenever we mention a speaking mouth, one thinks of natural gifts. If he does not, then he imagines that what has been said does not apply to him. He will try to serve God in other ways. He will thank God with his money, influence, and his example. This is good, but it will not free anyone from the obligation of fulfilling his calling to bring to God the sacrifice of the lips. One of the tokens of the coming of the Kingdom of God was that not only would the blind see but also the dumb would speak and praise God.

The grace of God does not just take the darkness from the eyes so that the soul can know Him. It also opens the mouth to praise Him. Not only is an unclean spirit cast out but also the demon that was dumb. Along with the Holy Spirit all the disciples were given a mouth to praise God. In heaven there are no dumb men. Every tongue praises God. The Christian whose tongue is not loosened or liberated is defective. He is lacking one of the most glorious capabilities of the new man.

There is no question as to whether you have a natural gift for speaking. Many people speak briefly and simply receive from grace the capacity for achieving great results with their small gift. It is not the beauty of the language. It is the power of the life and spirit that the blessing depends on. Let your desire to receive grace also become stronger, under a sense of your solemn obligation to praise God and make Him known. Let every experience of weakness and inability urge you to find confidence in the power and promise of God. Out of such desire and confidence let the prayer rise, "Lord, open Thou my lips; and my mouth shall show forth Thy praise." The answer will not be far off. This decision may cause you much conflict and perseverance. This rich petition is not learned in one day. The riches of grace are not exhausted in one day. Yet, if you have the desire, you will obtain the blessing. Therefore, every time we use the prayer, "Have mercy upon me, O God," let us also add the petition, "Lord, open Thou my lips;

and my mouth shall forth Thy praise."

Chapter 28

# THE SACRIFICE OF LOVE

*"For thou desirest not sacrifice; else would I give it: Thou delightest not in burnt offering"*—Psalm 51:16.

David has surrendered himself to God in the joy of deliverance and thanksgiving. From now on he will live to honor and praise God. Nevertheless, he feels how little he can do. The question arises within him, is there not something more the Lord desires from him? He thinks of sacrifices. By multiplying these could he not accomplish a work that would be acceptable to the Lord? As soon as the question arises, it becomes clear that God does not delight or have pleasure in sacrifices.

The clearness with which David feels and expresses this is one of the deep spiritual lessons of this psalm. In the hidden part, God has made him to know wisdom. He is more aware of his sin than ever before. He knows grace in its high spiritual power. He had experienced the wonderful work of God in forgiveness and renewal. He had learned to understand the symbolical sprinkling and washings of the Old Testament. He had experienced how God washes and purifies the soul. Now the Spirit has also unfolded to him the life of thankfulness and shown him how insufficient external sacrifices would be.

## Two Kinds Of Sacrifices

Under the old covenant there were two kinds of sacrifices: sin offerings and guilt offerings for atonement; thank offerings and burnt offerings to represent dedication to God. Discovering the depths of sin caused David to feel the need of something more than an external atonement. Now he understands that it is an inward, spiritual dedication that God wants from him.

In all these respects, this psalm is a prophecy of the grace of the New Testament. It is always in this statement, "Thou delightest not in sacrifice," that the difference between the Old and New Testament lies. Under the old covenant and according to the law, man must always bring God and give God something for taking away sin. In the gospel, on the other hand, God brings to man and gives him what can atone for sin. Under the old covenant, man must bring sacrifice to God in the hope that He receives it. Under the new covenant, God comes to man with a sacrifice, in order that he may receive it and be blessed.

This is the meaning of the word of the prophet repeated by Jesus when He said to the Pharisees, "But go ye and learn what that meaneth, I will have mercy, and not sacrifice" (Matthew 9:13). To require and bring sacrifices—that was the characteristic of the old covenant—but to show and receive mercy is the glory of the new covenant. So the one who would fully enjoy the salvation of the gospel must above all try to understand the words, "Thou delightest not in sacrifice."

## Mercy, Not Sacrifice

This word reminds us of the freedom of God's grace as a source of blessing. The spirit of law—righteousness and work-righteousness is so natural to us that we are inclined to see God as "a hard, austere man" who makes heavy demands on us. If we could only abandon this attitude. God is a God who does not demand but gives freely. The secret of fellowship with Him is always to look to Him as a God from whom one may ask and expect everything. He delights in mercy and not in sacrifice.

This is true of the first grace of forgiveness. How long did you think that there was something you had to do in order to receive God's grace? How long did you think there was something you had to bring and offer in order to be acceptable to God? When faith became plain to you as simply receiving what God had done for you and offered to you, your response was, "Is that all? Is salvation so near and so easy to find?" Then you learned what is meant by saying, "Thou delightest not in sacrifice."

The same thing is also true of the higher grace of santification. Holiness is not something we must accomplish. Holiness is only in God. We become holy only as He makes us share in His holiness. Christ has been given to us for justification, and sanctification. The one who understands that truth fully enjoys his salvation of the life of grace. He knows he no longer has to represent the life of divine salvation as a severe sacrifice, but as a glorious experience of what the grace of God works in him. Obedience is something higher than sacrifice. This deeply significant statement reveals the secret of the true service of God. It is not what man does or brings to God, but the childlike attitude of loving submission that is the true fulfillment of the law.

The believer who served God with difficulty and self-sacrifice can now discover the joy of the life prepared for him through the compassion of God in Christ. His service to God becomes a service in the joy of love. Love does not speak of sacrifices. Others may glory in the sacrifices which love brings, but love does not consider them to be sacrifices. They are a joy and a delight.

When we become aware of the gracious attitude of God toward us, we can apply this word to our relationships with other people, "I will have mercy, and not sacrifice." We can meet the unsaved with compassion and tenderness, not with the hard requirements of the law. We can understand the secret of the love by which transgressors learn God's ways, and sinners are converted to Him. "Thou delightest not in sacrifice" is the gospel of personal comfort which can be joyfully proclaimed to others.

## Chapter 29

# MAINTAINING A BROKEN SPIRIT

*"The sacrifices of God are a broken spirit: a broken and a contrite heart, O God, Thou wilt not despise"*—Psalm 51:17.

In the beginning of the psalm David had, out of his deep guilt, revealed that his heart was broken. We have seen that a contrite spirit is a definite characteristic of the person seeking grace. In the course of the psalm, however, David's tone undergoes a change. He has spoken of joy and gladness and has given promises full of courage and strength. You might think that a broken heart is necessary at first, but later on, when grace has done its work, this broken condition is no longer important. As a matter of fact, it is quite the contrary. Even in the life of grace, from the beginning to the end, God is especially pleased with the attitude of a broken and a contrite heart. This is an abiding and unmistakable feature of the life of thanksgiving which the Spirit wants us to experience. "The sacrifices of God are a broken spirit."

# The Broken Spirit

This statement teaches us how the broken spirit will, for the believer, always be a token of grace. God, according to His promise, forgets sin, but the believer never forgets it. Being a sinner is not something superficial and temporary. To maintain and enjoy the right kind of fellowship with the Lord, we must always be mindful of who we are and how much we are indebted to His grace. Just as the Lord said to redeemed Israel, "and I will establish My covenant with thee; and thou shalt know that I am the Lord: that thou mayest remember, and be confounded, and never open thy mouth any more because of thy shame, when I am pacified toward thee for all that thou hast done, saith the Lord God" (Ezekiel 16:62,63). It is not just the sense of guilt, but the power of grace and forgiving love that melts, humbles, and bruises the soul before God. Often, it is just the glorious proof of the goodness of God that overwhelms the soul and makes it remain contrite in the awareness of its own unworthiness.

God has no delight in sacrifice or pleasure in the greatest external offerings that may be brought to Him. His sacrifice is a broken spirit. It is on the inner man, the hidden man of the heart, that He looks. It is in spirit and truth that He wants to be worshipped. The sacrifice that He desires is a living, spiritual sacrifice. If we feel we have so little to bring to the Lord, this word comes with grateful comfort. "A broken and a contrite heart, O God,

Thou wilt not despise." This reminds us that the Lord never delights in anything as much as that feeling of emptiness and failure which breaks the soul. This feeling makes the heart capable of receiving and appreciating the wonderful grace of God. This feeling teaches us to look away from ourselves and seek everything in God. This contrite attitude gives glory to God alone. God bends over such a heart with inexpressible tenderness to gloriously fulfill the promises of His Word.

## The Contrite Heart

Read the great statements of Isaiah on this point (Isaiah 57:15, 66:1,2). There is no place in the world in which the holy God, when He stoops from His glory, will so readily set up His throne as *the contrite spirit*. He also devotes much work to the accomplishment of this bruising of the heart in His children. By the sense of guilt, the experience of sin, through many trials, and the work of the Spirit, God prepares His own for bringing to Him the sacrifice that pleases Him most—a contrite heart.

This verse further teaches us to understand how the freedom and joy of the life of grace will be manifested in the broken heart and the contrite spirit. This seems to be a contradiction. God's thoughts are not as our thoughts. The more we practice His Word, the more we will experience how our need and God's grace are bonded to one another. His life can then be fully revealed in our death. We will see His power in our weakness, His comfort in our sorrow, His help in our inadequacy, His healing in our oppression, and His love in our brokenness. We will also experience that the more we die to ourselves and yield ourselves to the discipline of the Spirit, the more God's good pleasure and His nearness to the broken in heart will become ours.

When you lift up the petition, "Have mercy upon me, O God," do not forget that this verse is closely connected with it. It is a word of anxiety but also a word of comfort. The value of this truth is felt in the confession of sin, the striving for holiness, the self-dedication of thanksgiving to praise God. "The sacrifices of God are a broken spirit." There is nothing in your Christian life that will enable you to find grace and influence with God and man as the holy ornament of a contrite spirit, which is of great price in the sight of God. "A broken and a contrite heart, O God, Thou wilt not despise."

## Chapter 30

# PRAYING FOR OTHERS

*"Do good in Thy good pleasure unto Zion: build thou the walls of Jerusalem"*—Psalm 51:18.

David began this psalm with prayer for grace for himself. However, he cannot end it with this same prayer. The blessed experience of grace makes him think not only of unbelievers, but also of the people of God who partake of this grace with him. For these he pours out his heart. He can never forget the city of God. This is an essential element of true prayer and a principal characteristic of the true believer. The true believer is also an intercessor. We should pay attention to the important lesson this verse teaches us.

## Learning To Pray

In the first place, true intercessors for the Church of God are those who have first learned to pray for themselves. Personal need is the school in which true intercessors are trained. It is in the confession of personal sins that the secret of believing intercession is learned. There are many in church and prayer meetings who pray for themselves and others, and yet they know little of personal communication with God in the prayer, "Cleanse me from my sin."

First of all, the sinner must feel as if he has God's undivided attention. He must learn to deal with God for himself alone. Then he will learn to understand the grace of God and know how to plead for this blessing on behalf of the people and the city of the Lord. Then, he not only obtains courage to speak of God to his fellow-men, but also delights in doing so. He also feels he has power to speak and plead with God on behalf of his fellow-men.

Those who have learned to pray for themselves become intercessors of their own accord. Grace is not self-seeking. The love of God shed abroad in the heart creates love in God's people and church. This is true of the nation of Israel. Think, for example, of the prayers of Ezra, Nehemiah, and Daniel (Ezra 9, Nehemiah 9, Daniel 9), or the way the converted Saul of Tarsus continually prayed for the early churches. Intercessors such as these are called "watchmen on the walls of Jerusalem" (Isaiah 62:6).

God makes us fellow-workers with Him, and He is prepared to listen to us, and at our urgent request He will answer. As soon as there are several in a church who, in their own experience, learn to understand the grace of God exhibited in this psalm, the prayer meeting will include the petition, "Do good unto Zion."

## Appealing To God's Compassion

It is not just the experience of deliverance from personal sin that motivates people to pray. There is something more. David felt himself to be one with the people. He was afraid his sin might possibly prove harmful to the city as a whole, so he prayed that any serious consequences might be averted. Aware of the terrible power of sin to destroy, the intercessor asks the Lord to turn aside the dreaded evil, and do good to Zion according to His good pleasure.

"Do good in Thy good pleasure unto Zion." It is to God's good pleasure in Zion that intercessors appeal when they ask Him to do good to her. The Psalmist appeals to God's lovingkindness and the greatness of His compassion for His people. David's knowledge of God's character gives him power and courage to pray. We should never forget this. Our strongest argument in prayer is the being and heart of God. The more we cling to what God has revealed concerning His feelings toward His people and His purposes and promises, the more we will feel the power to pray. The good pleasure of God toward Zion is the foundation for our hope, the measure of our expectations, and the strength of our faith. If our souls were more fully possessed by this conviction, we would pray more earnestly, "Do good . . .unto Zion."

This great overwhelming goodness is expressed in the words, "Build Thou the walls of Jerusalem."

That petition includes *building up* where they were not yet completed; *rebuilding* where they were broken down by hostile attacks; and *outbuilding* where they had become too narrow for the growing number of inhabitants. It includes prayer for the new spiritual growth of the congregation, for the maintenance of God's authority, and the extension of the Kingdom of God by the ingathering of those who do not know Him. The believer who has tried to understand God's plan for the heavenly city, will certainly feel how necessary this prayer is in our time. Zion, the city of God, the dwelling place of the Most High, will exhibit the splendor of the New Jerusalem (Revelation 21:10). In the midst of severe toil and conflict, disappointment and hindrances, living stones are being laid, and the walls slowly rise.

"Build Thou the walls of Jerusalem." Believers need to make this their prayer because of their unbelief and worldliness. In view of the needs of millions who do not know the Lord, let the grace shown to you cause you to pray, "Do good in Thy good pleasure unto Zion: build Thou the walls of Jerusalem."

## Chapter 31

## PLEASING GOD WITH OUR SACRIFICES

*"Then shalt Thou be pleased with the sacrifices of righteousness, with burnt offering and whole burnt offering: then shall they offer bullocks upon Thine altar"*—Psalm 51:19.

When God in His good pleasure will do good to Zion and build the walls of Jerusalem, a glorious time will dawn for the city and people of God. Then, says David, God will be pleased with the sacrifices brought to Him. Then, the people will also have delight and offer them with gladness upon the altar. In a preceding verse he said, "Thou desirest not sacrifice." Those words show the deep spiritual insight David had concerning the inferiority of the old covenant sacrifices. God could not desire these offerings because they were the work of man. God desired something higher and better in the all sufficient sacrifice of His Son (Hebrews 10:5-10). David now understands that when Zion is again visited by God He will again be pleased with the sacrifices of righteousness.

## Our Relationship To God

Very important lessons are taught us in this verse. First of all, we see how the worth of our religion depends entirely on our relationship to God. The very same psalm which says, "Thou desirest not sacrifice," says later, "Then shalt Thou be pleased with the sacrifices of righteousness." In the interval between these two statements, a great change has taken place. Since sin has been atoned for, the good pleasure of God must now rest upon Zion. Her sacrifices must be acceptable to Him.

The sacrifices are no longer brought to take away unrighteousness, but they are a symbol of the dedication and thanksgiving from a justified people. They are sacrifices that God can really "take pleasure in." This teaches us something about our fellowship with God. The value of all our works is defined by our relationship to God. If we are not reconciled to God, and have not received atonement and forgiveness of sins in Christ, then our best works cannot be pleasing to God. If, on the other hand, we have become the children of God and the relationship between Him and us is as it should be, then He takes delight in our service and works. They are acceptable to Him. It is said, in the words of David, "Thou desirest not sacrifices," but he also says, "Thou shalt be pleased with sacrifices." The same is true in the words of Paul. First we read, "Not of works," but he also writes, "Created unto good works" (Ephesians 2:9,10). The very same works that, before faith, are worthy to be rejected, are, after faith, an acceptable service to God.

## Pleasing Sacrifices

We must ask ourselves whether the Lord takes pleasure in our work. Is it pleasing to Him? Cain presented a sacrifice but God did not look upon his sacrifice. We can offer God our earnestness and zeal, but the great question is whether He takes delight in us and our sacrifice.

It is not how we pray and what we do that can bring us blessing. Instead, it is the fact that God accepts our praying and doing and sends an answer to it. Many remain content when they think they have done their best to serve God and obtain rest in this duty. With living faith this is not so. It will not merely set the wood in order and slay the victim, but it will crave the fire from heaven to consume the sacrifice. Living faith desires proof that the sacrifice is pleasing and acceptable to God. Living faith does not merely seek to serve God in the way that is ordained by Him. But it desires to know that God takes delight in our sacrifices. The tenderhearted believer must know that God is pleased with his sacrifice.

David's word teaches us further, that when God takes delight in the sacrifices of righteousness, His people will also take delight in them. *"Then* shalt Thou be pleased. . .then shall they offer bullocks.'' There is nothing that will create more joyful service than the blessed certainty that God is pleased. When we know that God is pleased with our effort and that every sacrifice is a joy to Him, the heart becomes strengthened to serve Him. The sacrifice itself becomes a joy and a delight. Yes, the secret of true Christianity is the joy of knowing that God delights in our sacrifices. *"Then shall we* offer bullocks upon Thine altar."

It will be a glorious time when, in the light of God's countenance, His people will joyfully and willingly dedicate themselves to Him. May we pray with new sincerity, "Do good in Thy good pleasure unto Zion: build Thou the walls of Jerusalem. Then shalt Thou be pleased with the sacrifices of righteousness. . .then shall they offer bullocks upon Thine altar." May we always approach God with the prayer, "Have mercy upon *me*, O God." May His answer strengthen us in the knowledge that God will deal with Zion and do good to her, and that the hour will be hastened when His Church will bear the name of Hephzibah, "My delight is in her" (Isaiah 62:4).